A Heart of Wisdom

Inspiration and Instruction for Conscious Elderhood

Anne Beattie-Stokes

To order additional copies, please contact us.
Booksurge Publishing
www.booksurge.com
1-866-308-6235
orders@booksurge.com

Scripture quotations are from the Holy Bible, New Revised Standard Version, New York: Oxford University Press, 1989, Division of Christian Education of the National Council of Churches in the United States of America.

All photographs and art in the book are by Anne Beattie-Stokes with the exception of the photograph on page 63, which was taken by Mary Margaret Farrow.

Unless otherwise noted, the poetry is by Anne Beattie-Stokes.

With gratitude
this book is dedicated to
Mickey Johnstone
whose wise heart
continues to inspire and instruct me
and
to all the wise teachers
who have graced my journey.

Contents

Introduction

An Invitation

A Heart of Wisdom is a book of inspiration and instruction for conscious elderhood. The photographs, art work, and poetry are meant to portray the joy and beauty, the awe and wonder, the hope and promise that are possible even amidst the terrors and troubles of growing old. They are meant to inspire you to undertake your journey. The text and the exercises are guidance for the way. They are meant to instruct you on your journey.

The idea for this book came about when my own life was rounding a corner into elderhood and my studies toward a Doctor of Ministry led me to the field of conscious elderhood. During this time, many events were bringing the issues of conscious elderhood alive in my own experience. One of these experiences was the final illness and death of my mother. Another was a Conscious Elderhood Vision Quest in Colorado and Utah, and yet another was an encounter with a dead doe in the pampas grass on Antelope Island in the Great Salt Lake.

These encounters and experiences, along with the research and reading I undertook for various assignments in the Doctor of Ministry program, have guided my own inner work and deepened my knowledge of conscious elderhood. Making art and writing poetry and elder tales brought insights from the unconscious to deepen my knowing. On every step of the journey, nature has been a guide, through its rhythm of birth, life, death, new life, teaching me to trust life's sure unfolding. Trees, particularly, offered their wisdom with generosity, and so the chapter headings are based on what trees know about life, aging, and death.

The culmination of this stage of my journey has been putting together this book which is intended for use by individuals who desire to engage the work of their own conscious elderhood. Some of the work may be done on your own; some may be done in groups who meet to support one another.

My own faith journey is that of a Christian who has come to an ecofeminist faith and theology. However, I respect every spiritual path as right for the person who follows it with integrity and trust. There is much in the book that will enable a person of any denomination or none, of any religion or none to follow his or her own path toward conscious elderhood.

The book begins with the story of my elderhood journey to this point. In my journey, perhaps you will find an opening to your own journey. In Chapter Two, I explore two metaphors of aging. One, *a heart of wisdom*, comes from scripture and gives this book its title. The other, *creating a safe place to die*, comes from my experience with the dead doe in the pampas grass on Antelope Island. Chapter Three explores metaphors of aging in nature. Chapters Four and Five explore a variety of practices for soul and spirit. These include circle, storytelling, ritual, soul poetry, dream work, and art and are the basis for the exercises in the book.

Chapters Five through Eleven provide the substance of the book. They describe the themes and tasks of conscious elderhood and offer exercises for you to deepen your inner work. One way to approach these chapters is to read them one at a time. Work through the material slowly, allowing it to make connections in your own experience and to illumine your own path. Depending on your personality, some exercises will appeal to you more than others. Some are easier and more attractive; some are more difficult and daunting. I encourage you to undertake some of each. Pushing your boundaries will help you grow. The energetic field of a group can help you deepen your work and keep you accountable to your own path and pace.

When you come to the end of the book, your journey of conscious elderhood is only beginning. Over time, you may want to revisit some of the themes and exercises, especially those which did not seem particularly germane to you on first reading. Conscious elderhood is a journey and the journey is all.

Along the way, the journey that has led me to this book has also led to many people who have helped me learn about the tasks of waking up to the terrible beauty of growing old.

The work of Animas Valley Institute and the people whom I have met through their programs, particularly my sisters and brother in the Soulcraft Immersion Program have taught me to dive into the darkness of soul and to rise on the wings of Spirit. [1]

Through them I have deepened in my own inner work and in my understanding of the role of nature, dream work, storytelling, circle, and ritual. These learnings are reflected in every word and image in this book, but especially in the chapters on practices for soul and spirit.

Five retired ministers of The United Church of Canada graciously took part in an applied research project into their experience of conscious elderhood. Individually and together they explored with me the landscape of growing old. From our shared work come the issues of elderhood which I discuss in the book: Facing Debility and Death, Doing Everything with Soul, Coming to Terms with our Lives, Discovering What We Yet May Be, Spirituality and Faith, and Gleaning and Passing on our Life's Wisdom. Some of the art work included in the book was my response to their stories. The five elder tales included in Appendix A were written as metaphors of their experience.

I also am grateful for the work of some of the members of White Oaks United Church who took time to respond to the art, photography, and poetry and to do some of the exercises found at the end of each chapter. Their responses about how the material inspired and instructed them in the work of their elderhood were crucial in deciding what should be revised, what should be included in the book, and what should be omitted.

The White Oaks congregation also gave me a three month sabbatical leave in which to complete not only my work on this book, but also the dissertation for my Doctor of Ministry. I am very grateful for their love and generosity and I look forward to growing old with them.

To my classmates Ted and Caryn in the Doctor of Ministry program at St. Stephen's College in Edmonton, Alberta and to the faculty of the college I also owe a debt of gratitude. They have encouraged me from the beginning and their insight and support along the way have kept me going.

Dr. Brenda Peddigrew has supervised all of my research projects and is the Chair of my Project/Dissertation Committee. Her unfailing encouragement and wisdom have guided each step.

Dr. Geoff Wilfong-Pritchard and Dr. Margaret Trapnell, the two other members of my Project/Dissertation Committee, have also given support and wise counsel.

In company with these wise teachers and companions, I invite you to dare the journey of consciousness in elderhood. As my mother used to say, "growing old is not for sissies," so I wish you courage and faith for the way.

May these words and images guide you on your journey so that you may get a heart of wisdom.

Notes:

Chapter One

The Journey of Elderhood Begins

> The compensation of growing old, Peter Walsh thought... was simply this: that the passions remain as strong as ever, but one has gained—at last!—the power which adds the supreme flavour to existence—the power of taking hold of experience, of turning it round, slowly, in the light. [2]
>
> Virginia Woolf, *Mrs. Dalloway*

As long as I can remember, my longing for God has been a longing to become wise. I have longed to live in such a way that I may "gain a wise heart." [3] I have longed to be able to hold my experience up to the light and learn from it to be more confident, more discerning, and more tolerant of myself and others.

I have longed to "grow up in every way... into Christ" whom I see as the epitome of wisdom. [4] In his acceptance of all people and in his open-hearted love of God, I see a person who has honoured every day by living with God, a person who is at peace with mystery and paradox, a person whose heart is full of compassion for *all* people—a person who has a heart of wisdom.

His is the kind of wisdom I long to develop and his is the humanity I will seek all my life to embody. As I move into my elderhood, I find that I am more able to integrate my life's experience with creativity, compassion, discernment, and tolerance, and that this is a strong base from which to wake into a wise heart in elderhood.

My journey of waking into wisdom in elderhood took a giant step forward when I started to be aware of the deep sadness I felt when I saw elderly people whose physical and mental powers were obviously waning. Their struggle with tasks that at one time would have been as easy as breathing broke my heart open to the inevitability of my own aging. Their vulnerability and diminishment hooked my own fears about growing old. Thus, sadness and fear were the voice of my soul calling me a first time to the work of consciousness *in elderhood*.

To My Mother, at 84

With pain and loss,
she comes to the end
of her life
and is diminished.
Fighting the indignity,
her anger swells,
becoming more,
while she is less.
This loss
of independence
galls and
frightens her.
The pain she bears
in bone and bygones
is changing her,
and that realization is
greater agony.
She has fewer
defences
to stem the flow
of feelings
that sweep over her.

The tide has turned;
flotsam and jetsam
are exposed
on the shore of her
life.
Broken shells
cut her feet.
Decaying matter
bloats and smells.
Wood from far
shores
bleaches in the sun—
the leavings of the
years

exposed
as life ebbs
to its close.

I stand helpless,
can only watch
and love
the changes,
try not to cut
my feet,
or wrinkle
my nose,
or stumble
over the debris
where we walk
together
on this bleak shore.

When the tide
ebbs,
she will board
the ship that waits,
and be borne
to the farther
shore
where life floods
in fullness,
eternally.

And I cannot
go with her
yet.

In 1998, Mom and I moved in together and I was privileged to share the last years of her life. As I watched her encounter the burning and blackening of her life and eventually her death, I was taught how essential it is to begin the work of getting a heart of wisdom before it is made a necessity by illness and loss. This time with my mother was the voice of my soul calling me a second time to the work of consciousness in elderhood.

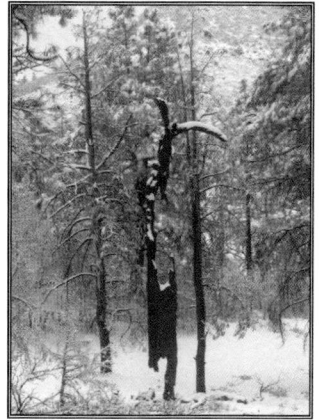

When Mom died in 2000, the last of her generation, my older brother said to my younger brother and me, "Now we're at the front of the church." My brothers and I are now the oldest generation in our family. In the natural order of things, we will be the next to die.

Around the time of my mother's death, I also began to notice that when I walked in nature what entered my awareness were things that were dead and dying. Everywhere, I saw trees, plants, and animals in various stages of decay and death. I looked into the mirror of nature and saw my own dying, and death in nature was the voice of my soul calling me a third time to the work of consciousness in elderhood.

Not long after these experiences, I discovered a poem by Dawna Markova called, "I Will Not Die an Unlived Life." [5] Markova's words captured beautifully my yearnings and fears about waking up into elderhood. To wake up into elderhood—to become a *conscious* elder—to get a heart of wisdom—is to learn to inhabit my days with courage and live, not from ego's smallness and fear, but from my soul's flaring forth. To become a conscious elder is to allow soul to break open my heart so that it flies, flames, and finds its fullness in the promise of abundant life in Christ.

To become a conscious elder is to risk living in such a way that the blessings I have received grow and are passed on in greater beauty, depth, and fruitfulness. It is learning to sing the *soul's* song: God's song of the wise heart, so that others may eat of the fruit of the tree of life in the garden that God has planted in my life.

Next, the work of becoming conscious in elderhood took me on a Vision Quest during which I gathered with men and women in the red rock canyon country of the Colorado plateau and then on a high mesa in the Utah desert. During the solo time of that quest, I camped on the rim of Arches canyon where I fasted alone for three days and three nights, calling for a vision that would enable me to grow old with attentiveness and courage. Out of these experiences, came an elder tale—a gift of wisdom to carry me into my elderhood.

The Woman Who Will Learn To Fly

A woman lived beside the forest and traveled there every day of her life to gather fire for her hearth and food for her table.

So familiar was she with the forest, that she knew every sound: the birds singing in the tree tops, the raccoon rustling his way home at dawn, the deer crashing through the brush at evening, the owl screeching in the darkness. She knew the forest and she loved it, and in turn the forest loved her, feeding her in body, soul, and spirit.

Then one day when her hair was growing grey, the woman entered the forest in search of food and fire wood. Maybe she was tired, for her stamina was not what it used to be. Maybe she lost her way, for her memory wasn't as sharp as it once was. Maybe she missed a path, for her eyesight was failing. Maybe it was magic or simply the turning of the great wheel of life. Whatever the reason, that day the woman went more deeply into the forest than ever before.

Suddenly, her awareness changed as if she were waking from a dream into day. For the first time in her long memory, the forest was silent. No bird sang from its hidden nest; no animal rustled through the underbrush. All was quiet and the woman was afraid. Quickly she turned to go back the way she had come, only to discover that the trees had closed in behind her. She could not go back, only forward.

Turning from the direction she had come, the woman saw that there were no trees in front of her anymore, only rock—rock and sand as far as she could see, and in the distance, a great way off, a mountain touched by the evening sun.

The woman had never seen anything so beautiful, so shining, so distant—so different from anything she knew. Again she turned to go back—back to the forest, back to what she knew and loved. But something about the shining mountain drew her, and she turned toward its strange, luminous presence.

"Your path lies onward," peeped a small voice.

"But I don't know the way. Nothing is familiar out there. The silence frightens me." Startled at her own voice, the woman realized with amazement that she was talking to a butterfly that was slowly fanning its blue, black, and white-patterned wings on a rock near her feet.

"I will show you how to ride the wind," said the butterfly, "all the way to the Sacred Mountain. Do not be afraid. The wind will carry you."

"But I will die out there," said the woman.

"Yes," came the reply, "But first, you will learn how to live."

The woman looked toward the Sacred Mountain shining above the now-dark desert, and said, "Then teach me to ride the wind. Teach me to live."

And the wind blew.

This tale grounds me in the learning of my earlier years and opens me to the wisdom of the heart. It reminds me that elderhood is a new land which requires death to the old ways of being so that a new way can unfold. The work of conscious elderhood is to create a safe place to die and then to let go.

This understanding was deepened through an encounter on Antelope Island in the Great Salt Lake. In a stand of pampas grass where I had spent time the day before in prayer and meditation, there was a dead doe who looked as if she had simply laid down to sleep. Her beauty and stillness, and the depths of her dark eyes drew me to her.

An active imagination dialogue with the doe revealed to me that the inner work I had done there in the grass had made it a safe place for her to die. This insight taught me that the work of waking up as an elder creates a safe place for me to die. It taught me that doing *my* work also creates a safe place for others to die.

This insight taught me that my ministry is to help people die in every stage of life—to faith that is too small, to self-images that are too small, to views of the world that are too small, to the stage of life that is ending, and finally to life itself.

My own journey toward conscious elderhood, then, has been teaching me about what it means to get a heart of wisdom and how to create a safe place to die, the twin themes that form the basis of this book.

Unexpected Snow

A late snow in the Abajo Mountains covered spring flowers with snow.

What parts of you feel as though they are still blooming in the spring of your life, even though the winter of age is upon you?

The Path through the Autumn Woods

Where are you on the elderhood path?

Are you moving through autumn or are you already deep into winter?

Notes:

Chapter Two
Metaphors of Aging in Scripture and Experience

A Heart of Wisdom—A Metaphor from Scripture

Wisdom does not simply accrue to us through an accumulation of years. We become wise, scripture teaches us, by taking account of the limited number of our days. We become wise by living in the awareness that in the divine order we are promised life in all its fullness, but that abundant living is not a given. Rather, it is a conscious choice.

Wisdom is painstakingly gathered through reflection on our life experience and through the integration of our learning into the living of our lives. As Christians, we call this work theology, and the most vital source of theologizing is our experience.

> **What I am Becoming**
>
> Crinkly skin
> and sagging flesh
> stare at me
> from the mirror.
> I am becoming
> my mother,
> and it is good.

Our experience and how we see God at work in that experience come first and this leads to reflection on God's essence. As a first step in doing theology, we ask, *"What is my experience? What is God doing in my/our lives? and Where is God at work in our lived experience?"* Reflection on these questions leads us to ask, *"Who and what is God?"*

One day, in the course of writing this book, I stumbled into the bathroom without my glasses and looking into the mirror, I saw my mother looking back at me. There, on my face, was Mom's crinkly skin, on the backs of my arms her sagging flesh. I was face to face with my own aging.

Reflecting on the experience, I remembered divine goodness in all the days of Mom's life, even the sad and lonely ones, even the dark and painful ones. I remembered, if vaguely, words of scripture about God being with us, even to old age and grey hairs. Remembering, I was able to trust that when I am aware of the presence of the Great Mystery, becoming my mother is a good thing.

Our culturally-situated lives are the *text*, and the Bible and Christian tradition then become the *context* for reflection. So as we move into elderhood, we ask, *"What is my experience of growing older and where is God at work in that experience?"* Then we turn that experience around in the light that comes from scripture and tradition. Out of that reflection, we then ask, *"Who is God in this experience of growing old?"*

As we age in Western societies, we begin to identify with the dispossessed and with those who suffer. We begin to understand, perhaps for the first time, the experience of powerlessness, the experience of being disregarded and even feared, and the experience of being without a voice. We know in a new way what it means that, in Jesus, God shared the vulnerability and weakness of our humanity.

Our strength is waning; we begin to suffer illness and chronic pain; we no longer contribute to society through paid work; our children are grown and gone; our dreams have passed their best-before date; our financial resources are fewer, and our world begins to close in. Within ourselves, we may feel young and vigorous, but in a society which does not value either the wisdom of elders or the physical nature of old age, we may feel displaced and without worth.

Yet it is out of this very experience—*because of this experience and not in spite of it*—that we can get a heart of wisdom. The nearness of death teaches us about life and accepting our mortality frees energy for living. Letting go of our preoccupation with doing, we learn to live soulfully in the moment. This conscious living enables us to recover wonder, awe, and gratitude. Processing our life experiences and relationships leads to forgiveness, tolerance, and compassion.

Contemplation of our beliefs about God, Jesus, the after-life, and meaning and purpose moves us into deeper awareness of the Divine. We learn that faith is not about what we know, but who we know, and we recognize that even though we know less about the fullness of God's nature, we know God more fully because we are moving more deeply into oneness with the One.

Pondering our unlived dreams and exploring lost parts of ourselves compel us to continue learning and growing. Not wanting our lives to be in vain, we seek ways to glean the wisdom of our life experience and to pass it on as a legacy to others. For the sake of the future, we continue to try to make a difference.

And so, by deepening our consciousness in elderhood and doing the psychological and spiritual tasks of this stage of life, we count our days in such a way that we may get a heart of wisdom.

A Safe Place to Die—A Metaphor from Experience

It was during a retreat on Antelope Island in the Great Salt Lake that I was awakened to the awareness that one of the themes of conscious elderhood is creating a safe place to die. At the time, I was undergoing a huge transformation in my own faith and spirituality and it was through the experience on Antelope Island that I began to understand this change more fully and to have the courage to let go into the new life that was presenting itself to me.

On the second day of our retreat, our guides asked us to go out onto the salt flats to begin work on a "soul canvas"—a history of our numinous and luminous experiences—our encounters with the Divine Mystery and its unfolding in our lives. While looking for a place on the flats that would be big enough to hold the story of my journey with God and the unfolding of my being, I found a glass milk bottle from Cloverleaf Dairy in Salt Lake City. It was encrusted with salt, but still beautiful, and I decided to keep it as a souvenir. Only later was it pointed out to me that Cloverleaf is the name of the road where our cottage is situated among the beautiful rocks and trees of Haliburton County.

When it was time to head back to the campsite, I foolishly decided to go through the pampas grass that fringes the salt flats rather than hike the long way around. I had only gone about ten feet, however, when the grass, which was up to my chin, closed in around me. On every side, grasses with stalks as big around as my thumb lay tangled impenetrably across my path, while their flower-plumes rained down dusty seeds on my head.

In order to keep moving, I had to lift the grasses up and move them aside with my arms, and stomp them down with my feet. At one point, I looked down and saw that blood was pouring down my leg where a leaf had sliced my thigh. Soon I was sweating, breathing hard, and bleeding. Seeds from the grass were sticking to my sweat and blood and I fell.

As the grass closed over my head, thoughts of being lost forever swam through my mind and I wondered how I would ever be able to get back on my feet. I had the milk bottle in one hand and my water bottle in the other, and I didn't want to lose either one. This made standing up rather difficult and I was more than a little panicked. Eventually, though, I was able to stand, fight my way through the grass, and push my way out still holding the water bottle *and* the milk bottle.

They say that nothing happens by coincidence, and that it is the Divine energy in the Universe which makes things coincide and which is in all creation waiting to speak. So that night, in our circle, when I told the story of my time in the grass, I was encouraged to go back the next day to try and discover what this experience symbolized at this stage on my journey of life and faith. I was invited to ask myself these questions:

Who are the trapped ones of me?
Who are the bleeding ones of me?
What is being seeded in my sweat and blood?

The Question
When all the while
this tangle of grasses
within has
trapped
and cut
the inner ones of me,
whom have I been unwilling to
meet?

In my tent later that night, in a desert silence punctuated by the howling of coyotes, I prayed about the experience and asked for clarity about the questions I would take back into the grass.

The next morning, I made a little nest in the grass where I prayed, meditated, and sang. I asked to meet the ones of me who had been trapped within and not allowed, yet, to live the fullness of their being. I asked about the bleeding ones of me who had been wounded by my fear.

I also asked about the significance of the milk bottle and the water bottle that I had been carrying in the grass and discovered that they were significant symbols of my spiritual journey. They represent the two paths I have been travelling: the two faces of my spirituality, two paths to the Divine, two ways of knowing God and growing in faith and compassion.

For years, it has been increasingly clear to me that the new cosmology, the story of the formation of the Universe and the flowering of life on Earth must somehow to be harmonized with the Christian story and Christian theology. Here was an opening to a new understanding.

The milk bottle represents the nourishment of the mother—all the ways that mother Earth, and indeed the whole Universe, nurture my soul and speak of God and of my own deepest truth. The water bottle represents Jesus Christ who is a source of living water, and symbolizes all the stories, sacraments, and rituals of the Christian tradition. Combining these two life-giving streams, it seemed to me, was the way to deep inner healing of self, community, and the Earth itself.

Combining these two streams was the way to a vibrant, living faith for our time, and to a love that is big enough to embrace the whole world. I was being called to find ways to integrate these two streams in my own spiritual life and in my ministry, and it seemed to me that the connection between water and milk is the body—the body of the Earth and my body. How to make this connection remained a mystery.

The next day, the answer to the mystery came through the encounter with the dead doe which I described earlier. I was being called to create a safe place for people to die. Milk and water, soul and spirit, nature and the Divine were to be the means of doing this work. Dying and rising, in nature and in Christ, were to be both meaning and means for waking up in life and in elderhood.

The Pampas Grass

Those who become conscious in elderhood create a safe place to die by facing our mortality. Throughout our lives, all of us have lived the rhythms of morning and evening, spring and winter. We have seen how seeds fall into the ground and then burst forth as new shoots. We have seen young trees growing in fallen logs and dead stumps. We know that a snake sheds its skin in order to grow and that bodies decay into the earth and become fertilizer for other living beings. If we have been paying attention, we know that dying and rising form the very matrix of our own lives.

We have all experienced relationships taking root, coming to fullness, bearing fruit, and then withering. We have seen dreams die and new ones rise from the ashes. We have been part of organizations which flourished and then died slow deaths. We have worked and retired, and lived through the stages and seasons of our lives. We have experienced a presence greater than our own in these dyings and risings, and have learned to trust that death and resurrection are at the very heart of the divine life. We have learned that even though the process of dying may be fraught with confusion and contradiction, with chaos and fear, with decay and a sense of abandonment, we can trust that death gives way to life. We have learned to trust the rhythm of dying and rising and we know that this trust creates a safe place to die.

Carrying with us our trust in the divine energy of living and dying, we create a safe place for our physical death. This work involves practices which transform the values, deep beliefs, and guiding images that make up our personal myths of death. This work creates a safe emotional, psychological, and spiritual place for our dying. We learn to meet death as we have met life, with awareness and courage, with a sense of adventure and gratitude, and with trust in the life to come, whatever form it may take.

Two Ways of Waking Up

Without me hardly noticing, scripture and experience have become intertwined in my understanding of conscious elderhood. The metaphors of a heart of wisdom and a safe place to die, one from scripture and the other from experience, stand for me as an affirmation of my journey. Both metaphors point to ways of deepening into the journey of waking into elderhood. Both signify the presence of the Divine in the process of becoming wise and in all the places in life where we need a safe place to die into life.

Still Waters

Is there an image from scripture that reflects your experience of elderhood?

Where do you sense the river of experience flowing in elderhood?

Notes:

Chapter Three
Metaphors of Aging in Nature

Many of us are pagans at heart, encountering and praising God in creation and finding in nature the grounding of our experience of the Divine. Scripture affirms this experience and revelation of God in nature.

Psalm 19 says,

> "The heavens are telling the glory
> of God;
> and the firmament proclaims
> his handiwork.
> Day to day pours forth speech,
> and night to night declares
> knowledge.
> there is no speech, nor are there
> words;
> their voice is not heard;
> yet their voice goes out through
> all the earth,
> and their words to the end of
> the world. [1]

Like the psalmist, poets know that the Divine speaks in the voices of all the beings of creation.

Mockingbird in the Ocotillo

> I heard the voice of mockingbird
> in the ocotillo
> proclaiming the first lesson.
> "Sing to God all the earth.
> Sing to God all your songs."
>
> And I remembered other voices—
> loon and white pine,
> river and heron—
> God's other bible.

Unlike poets and psalmists, much of Christian theology dismisses the attribution of language to creatures as animism or pantheism. Yet it is possible, and even desirable, to enlarge our theological understanding to include the idea that the earth wakes us up to the Other: to the Divine as manifest in sky, river, rock, heron, and flying squirrel.

Further, just as our relationships with different people bring out different parts of ourselves, so a conversation with one of the Earth's beings makes visible parts of our unique being that we might not encounter in any other way.

We might begin deepening into the Divine in nature by developing a practice of walking in creation with the expectation of hearing the voices of other beings. Then we might find ways of listening to those voices that fit our spirituality and our person. Walking meditatively in nature, we will then find that we are in tune with the divine presence that is always seeking communion with us, and one of nature's beings draws our attention.

Then a conversation begins in which we learn about the other and perhaps about God and our own soul. In just such a conversation, a white pine mirrored to me its gladness in being itself and drew out my own longing to live the fullness of my soul.

Who actually did the speaking is not important because the Spirit of God moves in our hearts to draw us closer and to bring us clarity about the matters of the soul. White pine was the voice of the Divine calling me into the fullness of my self. Mockingbird was the voice of the Divine speaking of the necessity of singing to God all my songs. And whether the voice was mine or white pine's or mockingbird's, it was still God's voice. The Divine and the human, God and our deepest selves speak through all creation and those who want to become conscious would do well to listen.

Images of Aging in Nature

As we move into our elder years, we find many images in nature which mirror to us our own nature. By contemplating these images in creation, we see our own experience more clearly and can be present to it with awareness. In the following pages are some images from nature which speak to me of the realities of aging. Spend some time with each of these images and allow them to speak to you of your own experience and teach you about how to embody the wisdom of elderhood in a conscious way.

Peace at the Last

Day gives way to night with peace born of right timing and a sense of the goodness of the divine created order. All things end in their time, and letting go opens us to the peace that comes with acceptance.

Reflect on your experience of letting go.

Weathering to Wisdom

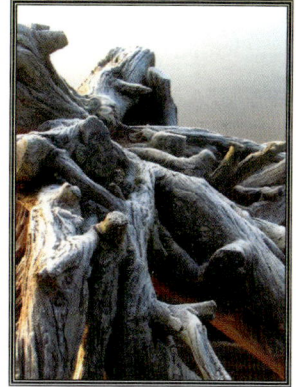

By the time we reach our elder years, we have weathered many life experiences. Our faces and hands carry the signs of our physical weathering, and our souls bear the beauty of experience that has weathered to wisdom.

Reflect on your feelings about how your body is weathering as you age.

Reflect on the way that your soul has weathered through all the many experiences of your life.

New Life from the Old

All life moves through cycles of birth, life, death, and new life. The new is always being born from the old.

Reflect on the times you have experienced new life rising from the old. What does this teach you in your elderhood?

**Bent by Storms—
Still Growing
to the Light**

In some season of its life, this birch tree was hit by an early snow that came while the leaves were still on its branches. The weight bent it to the ground, but did not break it.

In response to its new state, the birch began to send branches straight up toward the light so that they grew like new young trees out of the trunk of the old.

Reflect on how you adapted your life to new circumstances, and what this experience holds for you as you face the changes that come in old age.

Fallen Leaves

Reflect on what has fallen or is falling in your life as you age.

What is being swept away on the waters of time and old age?

In Light and in Shadow

Both light and shadow have their own deep beauty. Darkness reveals light that has been hidden. Dawn brings light to the night of sorrow. The rhythm of life is measured in light and shadow.

Reflect on the rhythm of light and shadow in your own experience. When have you walked in shadows? Were you aware of light in the darkness? When have you walked in light? What do you bring from these experiences into old age?

Reflect on the beauty and the terror of light and shadow as you approach elderhood.

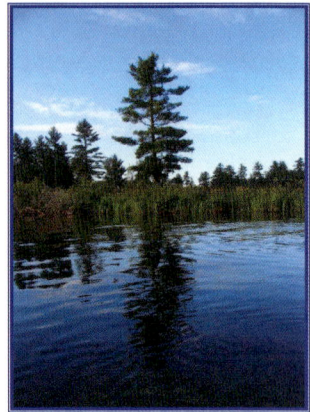

The Seasons of our Lives

For everything there is a season, and in old age, the season is winter. Throughout our lives, however, we have known the turning of the seasons. From stage to stage of life and within each stage itself, we have known the experience of birthing and greening, waning and falling, barrenness and new life.

Reflect on what have the seasons of your life taught you about winter. How are you carrying this experience of winter into your elderhood?

How are you experiencing spring, summer, and fall in the time of your elderhood?

Nature-based Practices

1. Attentiveness Walk
   Take a walk in nature and tune into your senses.
   Be aware of what you see, smell, feel.
   Let your thoughts pass over you like clouds over mountain.
   Note what you feel in your body.
   Notice your feelings.

2. Walking as the Child of You
   After about 15 minutes of walking attentively in nature, change your focus.
   As you walk feel yourself going back in time to become your child self. See and feel in a child-like way.
   Explore; feel; taste; examine everything with curiosity.
   Jump in mud puddles; lie on the ground on your back and watch the clouds.

3. The Walk of Three
   With each step, look at the ground in front of you and notice three things.
   Pay attention to what's under your feet.
   Keep doing this for at least half an hour. Take note of changes in your awareness as well as in your feelings.

4. Talking with Sacred Other
   Take a walk in nature and pay attention to what you see.
   When something grabs your attention, introduce yourself.
   Tell your story to the other.
   Then listen for what the other has to tell you.

5. Go out onto the Land
   Take an issue or emotion or a dream or a memory out onto the land.
   Look for that feeling, dream figure, or person in the land.
   Spend time in the presence of that being.
   Introduce yourself, have a conversation.
   Listen for its wisdom.

Notes:

Chapter Four
Practices for Soul and Spirit

In this book, I understand soul as the unique essence of anything: rock, tree, river, snowflake, human, organization, or community. It is the place of our deepest conversation with the world, the place of our destiny, the place where we learn to embody our true gifts and offer them back to the world in service of others. Soul is the diverse and multiple expression of the Divine in all of creation and in every manifestation of human life.

Although St. Paul writes about gifts, and Christian theology has explored the concept of gifts, the church has not been very adept at helping people to discover their unique way of being in the world which is the true gift that they can offer. We talk about gifts, but are not very skilled at enabling people to do the dark work of the soul journey which takes us into the Shadow where much of our beauty and giftedness lies hidden and dormant.

In this book, I understand Spirit as the One: the Divine which is transcendent and immanent in everything, the reality in which everything lives and moves and has its being. The journey to Spirit is a path of ascent on which "we *surrender* attachment to individuality and learn to transcend *both* ego identification and soul embodiment, ultimately seeing through the illusion of a separate self. We ascend toward an ecstatic merging with the Infinite, the Eternal, the Absolute." [1]

For much of its history, the Church has seen the journey toward the Divine Spirit as its primary task and has neglected the downward journey toward the Divine in the uniqueness of each soul. As a result, letting go has often come to mean denying one's true self as fallen and sinful, rather than embodying our unique soul in all its brokenness and beauty. In my understanding, we fully embody and then transcend rather than deny self.

As well, the Divine in nature has been minimized. As a result, very few Christians understand how creation participates in and embodies God in ways that teach us about ourselves and about our oneness with God and with all creation. We need to travel in the world of Spirit as those who know this oneness: those who are embodying and at the same time letting go of our own uniqueness.

The Characteristics of Soul and Spirit Practices

Practices for soul and spirit are **experiential.** They are based upon personal, unmediated experience. They embrace and value all our experience as human beings—our hopes and dreams, our disappointments and failures, our profoundest acts of creativity and compassion, as well as our deepest brokenness and pain. They embrace and value all the experiences of masculine and feminine consciousness, whether in men or in women or in creation.

Practices for soul and spirit are **creation-based.** They celebrate the mystery of the Cosmos, and the uniqueness of the self and of all beings as diverse manifestations of the same divine reality. They hearken to the words of scripture:

> Ask the animals, and they will teach you; the birds of the air, and they will tell you; ask the plants of the earth,
> and they will teach you; and the fish of the sea will declare to you. [2]

> The heavens are telling the glory of God;
> and the firmament proclaims [God's] handiwork. [3]

> Go to the ant, you lazybones;
> consider its ways, and be wise. [4]

These practices give attention to the paradox of creation's terrible beauty and seek to hold together grace and terror in the holiness of the Cosmos. They seek the Divine within us by awakening us to the beauty, pain, and wisdom of Earth, so that beauty breaks our hearts with longing, pain breaks our hearts with lament, and wisdom opens our hearts to compassion.

Practices for soul and spirit are **communal.** They acknowledge the integral fabric of our communion with Earth as the basis of our lives and as the source of our healing. They recognize that full human maturity and wholeness entail coming into relationship, and that none will be whole until all people and Earth and all its beings are whole. They recognize that there will be justice for no one until there is justice for all.

Practices for soul and spirit are **inward and outward**. They recognize that nature is within us in the form of archetypes, images, and symbols, and so these practices move us inward, believing that conversations with sacred other can heal our inner wounds and reveal the gifts that we are to bring to the world. These practices also lead outward to active commitment to a new order of justice in the world—an order which preserves the legacy of nature and the rights of the individual to fulfillment and happiness.

Practices for soul and spirit enter **solitude** in order to wait empty-handed for the present. These practices are based upon paying attention, listening and watching, and being in the moment. They arise from the hallowing of the everyday, and from apprehending the divine presence as the source of healing and hope in the beauty and brokenness, the gentleness and cruelty of ordinary moments. Practices for soul and spirit are those that enable us to wait alone in creation or in silence for a word or a hallowing, for meaning, awe, guidance or wisdom.

Practices for soul and spirit are **holistic.** They are based on the simultaneous and interpenetrating relationship of masculine and feminine, matter and spirit, finite and infinite. They seek unity in diversity and, as Christian practices, they find in Christ the centre in whom all things hold together and in whom transforming power transcends differences while sustaining the uniqueness of all things. The Divine is wholly transcendent *and* utterly immanent in the bodies of women, men, Earth and all its creatures.

Practices for soul and spirit are **embodied**. They remember that "the Word became flesh and dwelt among us," and hallow our own flesh and the Divine in all flesh. [5] Soul and spirit practices get us into our bodies so that we can access wisdom stored in our fibres and cells. They allow us to get out feelings we have pushed down into our bodies, and to love the body which sustains our life.

Soul and Spirit Practices

Circle

> Many of us who sit in circle regularly have come to
> see council as a spiritual practice, whether the
> circle is comprised of many dealing with
> community concerns or just two people exploring
> the mysteries of intimate relationship. By spiritual
> we do not mean to suggest a connection to any
> particular tradition or doxology. For us, a spiritual
> practice is any activity that both awakens the desire
> for, and provides the means to expand
> consciousness of Self, Other, and the Larger
> Mystery. [6]

The practice of circle, a way of speaking and listening together
in a group, is an excellent tool for elderhood groups because it
enables elders to ground their lives and their conversations in
wisdom that derives from the very nature and structure of the
universe. The practice of circle finds its energy in interdependence
and communion. It values diversity in oneness and seeks the
multiplicity of voices and opinions that leads to wholeness.

The practice of circle is inclusive, participatory, and mutually
respectful. It embodies the values of the reign of God in which
everyone has a voice and in which everyone contributes their gifts
and ideas for the well-being of the whole. The practice of circle is
experiential and communal. It enables people to find and value
their own voices and speak their truth, and it can therefore be an
agent of healing for elders who feel powerless, worthless, or
marginalized.

The practice of circle invites elders into silence where they can
touch their deepest wounds, know themselves as unique
embodiments of the Divine, and discover how they are meant to
use their gifts in their elder years.

Circle can be used to hone issues, resolve conflict, call for a
vision, and make decisions—all of which are tasks that couples,
families, and groups have to undertake at various times. Because of
its embodiment of the unity and diversity of the Cosmos, its
valuing of the wisdom and experience of the individual, and its
commitment to hearing all voices, the circle is a soul and spirit

practice which can help elders discern their soul gifts and calling and discover how they can bring those gifts to their community. Circles offer a safe place for dream work, storytelling, soul poetry.

Storytelling

> Whenever a [story] is told, it becomes night. No matter where the dwelling, no matter what the time, no matter the season, the telling of tales causes a starry sky and a white moon to creep from the eaves and hover over the heads of the listeners. Sometimes, by the end of the tale, the chamber is filled with daybreak, others times a star shard is left behind, sometimes a ragged thread of story sky. And whatever is left behind is our bounty to work with, to use toward soul-making." [7]

Christianity has a rich tradition of story, but most often we have told stories in order to learn about God. As a soul and spirit practice, we tell stories, not only to encounter the Divine, but for healing the souls of women and men, young and old, and Earth.

We tell stories which contain archetypal images that activate energy for a fuller living of our lives. Biblical stories often carry archetypal images such as ascent/descent, death/resurrection, elder, and hero, but these stories usually have been told to help us know God more fully and not always so that we recognize and affirm our own experience.

The story of Jonah, for example, has been a story of the God who calls and punishes the disobedient, when it could also be told as a story about what happens when we flee the hero's journey. In this kind of telling, Jonah's story shows us what happens when we try to avoid the journey of individuation—we end up in the belly of the beast.

Stories are experiential; they help us elders to reflect on our own experience as we face our mortality, come to terms with our lives, rediscover awe and wonder, discover what we yet may be, redefine our faith, and glean and pass on our life's wisdom.

Stories help us think about our relationship to the mystery of the Cosmos by speculating on questions of ultimacy, genesis, and eschatology. Christian creation stories locate us in the context of the meaning discovered in the God revealed in Jesus Christ. They make sense of the Cosmos in relation to the God of creation and stand in relation to the Cosmos through that God.

Stories, particularly those of indigenous cultures, connect us to the luminosity and holiness of the Earth. In Apache stories, it is the land which teaches the people how to live together in harmony. Through stories, elders, who have a vital role to play in protecting and advocating for Earth, learn how to live in right relationship to Earth and its other-than-human creatures. Stories show us how the land helps us come close to the mystery of our own embodiment of the Divine.

Stories also help us to make visible our community. "Who one is is in part defined by *whose* one is—to whom or what communal purposes one subscribes." [8] In the stories of scripture, we learn what it means to live as God's people in community and how to form our lives to the unity and diversity, multiplicity and oneness of the Universe—the design of the Cosmos that is within us and all around us, waiting to be fulfilled.

Stories remind us that we are connected to one another in the web of life and that we are called to shape our relationships with one another and with Earth to the mutuality, interdependence, and communion that are the very structure of the Universe.

Stories are also good for elders, because they get us out of ourselves. They allow us, if only for a while to try on other personae and practise being the ones of ourselves who were lost along the way. They let us laugh and cry and share in community.

Stories teach elders in western society how to be old in a way that is counter-cultural. They reveal elders who are vital and alive, and who are offering the gift of their wisdom for the sake of their communities.

"Given that the soul prefers to speak in images and symbols, poetry—our own and others—is a natural pathway to soul. Poetry, 'soul speech,' brings together the linguistic, linear part of the psyche with the imaginal, holistic part, enlisting the thinking mind in the service of soul, image and feeling. By immersing ourselves in the rich symbols of verse, we enhance the ego's ability to converse with soul." [9]

The language of poetry is at once open-minded and mysterious, revealing and hidden, rooted in the senses and imbued with soul and spirit. It has rhythm, shape, texture, and sound that are able to evoke experience. The language of poetry invites the soul to become visible and goes into hidden depths, where it stirs an inner recognition of what is made manifest.

The language of poetry also connects humans with the earth and enables us to hear the wisdom of Grandmother Earth and her beings, and to enter into a living relationship with the Divine in ourselves and in all beings.

For these reasons, Soul poetry is an excellent tool for elders, whether one is listening to it or creating it. It is particularly effective to use poetry in small groups of elders as a means of opening to soul. In his book, *A Hidden Wholeness,* Parker Palmer tells about the use of poetry in circles of trust, and points to ways that it can be used in the work of conscious elderhood. [10]

He says that the soul is shy and needs to be approached slant-wise—explored by means of a poem, a work of art, or a piece of music. At first, he says, it seems that we are talking about the artist's issues, but we soon become aware that we are really talking about ourselves. In this way, we can hold ourselves at whatever distance feels comfortable and reveal only what we choose, creating a safe place for the soul. The focus, however, is actually on how the poem intersects with our lives and evokes our experience of life in elderhood.

In an elder group which I am facilitating, I have used Dawna Markova's poem, "I Will Not Die an Unlived Life." As we discussed these lines in the group, we explored the legacy we want to leave through our lives, the fear both of failure and of our own power that has dogged us, and how we might increase our freedom to risk as we grow older. The poem helped us to make our elder challenges and passages more visible.

Another way to use soul poetry on our elderhood journey is to write our own poems. "One creative act can cause a torrent to break through stone," and lead us to deeper insights about our own lives and about the Divine in and around us. [11] Writing poetry can be done in small groups as a response to scripture or story. It can be done in our quiet time in response to prayer or meditation.

Writing poetry can also be a response to going out into nature and listening to the voices of Grandmother Earth's other beings. Haiku, Sonnet, and Villanelle, with their strict forms, are very useful for these types of exercise, as is simple free verse.

In these ways and others, elders use soul poetry as a means of making our passion, needs, powers, and commitment visible to ourselves. "Not only is the soul content to listen to [and create] this poetry, it is also encouraged to speak up, to join in, to sing its own song." [12]

Old Maude

A wooden rowboat,
its seams burst,
is tied at the dock,
full to the gunwales
with sun-warmed water.

A small girl plays inside.

With legs and body
slid under seats and thwarts,
she is held, lying
warmed
in a womb of water.

Rocking
wild and wondering,
drifting
silent and soaring,
she is a universe,

tied to a dock.

Now, in old age,
I am that child,
no longer tied,
but free again
for wonder.

Exercises for Storytelling and Soul Poetry

1. Elder Tales

   In a group of elders, read aloud one of the elder tales from Appendix A or a story from *In the Ever After* by Chinen. Read the selection aloud a second time, inviting participants to say, "Please stop!" when they come to a word or phrase or idea which raises a question or speaks to their experience in some way.

   Enter into a circle sharing in which each person who wishes has an opportunity to speak.

   When everyone who wishes has had an opportunity to speak, continue reading until once again someone says, "Please stop!"

2. Poetry

   With ritual, invoke a circle. In a group of elders, read aloud a poem from this book or by a "soul" poet like Mary Oliver, David Whyte, T.S. Eliot, Antonio Machado, Lorna Crozier, Rumi, Rainer Maria Rilke or W.H. Auden.

   In the circle, invite each person to speak about how this poem intersects with their own life.

   This is not a time for learned discussion, but for speaking and listening from the heart.

The Challenges of Elderhood

Notes:

Chapter Five
More Practices for Soul and Spirit

Ritual

Ritual "is a gathering with others in order to feel the Spirit's call, to express spontaneously and publicly whatever emotions need to be expressed, to create with others an unrehearsed and deeply moving response to Spirit, and to feel the presence of the community, including the ancestors throughout the experience." [1]

Ritual combines body, imagery, thought, feelings, and action in ways that make visible the sacred source of life, our connectedness in community, the diversity and unity of the Universe, the mystery of Spirit, as well as the stirrings of the individual soul.

The smoke of the Lakota pipe ceremony, for example, makes visible the invisible air, the breath of the Spirit, and the rising prayers of the people. The passing of the pipe—with each person breathing the sacred smoke—makes visible the connection among all people and beings. The ritual action combines collective meanings and forges individual identity within the community.

According to Stephen Gilligan, there are four kinds of ritual—transition, continuity, healing, and atonement. [2] As elders we need them all. We need rituals to mark our transition into elderhood, rituals to remind us of enduring truths of self and God that continue throughout life, rituals to heal the wounds of the past, and to make atonement for past wrongs.

When we engage in conscious rituals, we send the energy of image and symbol to the unconscious where transformation occurs at the deep place where meaning-making has its source. Conscious rituals are those which engage not only the mind, but the whole being, and particularly the body.

In creating such rituals, elders will involve the body and all the senses, so that the dualism of spirit and matter can be entered into and unity can be experienced. As appropriate, such rituals might include movement, gesture, dance, drumming or rattling. They might include texture, anointing, or washing. Such rituals might incorporate the sound of water splashing, of birds singing, or of thunder booming, as well as the sound of a drum or a singing bowl. Rituals will play with colours, shapes, symbols, and light—all the infinite variety and beauty of Earth that are sources of healing and hope.

"Living symbols...can initiate us into the mysteries of our own soul," so when we become conscious in elderhood, we learn to create our own rituals.[3] We listen to communication from nature, from our deepest selves, and from the Divine, and we learn how to use symbols from nature, from dreams, and from our daily lives in ritual that deepens us into our elderhood.

We learn how to create ritual space, "a place outside the ordinary, a place that looks and feels like an oasis in the middle of the desert." [4] We learn how to create a ritual beginning which acknowledges the transition to sacred space and sets the intention for the ceremony. We become skilled at creating the ritual action itself which symbolizes the conversation with soul or spirit, and we learn how to end a ritual with words of gratitude for what has happened and through words or action that shift us back to ordinary time and space.

When we as conscious elders create our own rituals, we can bring to community rituals greater consciousness which can increase the connectedness among people and the effectiveness of ritual for all who gather.

In the community and in individual lives, ritual can create a sense of home and belonging, cleanse and reconcile, develop inner knowing, and reconnect us to the wonder and beauty of creation and our place in it.

Through ritual, we make visible the sacred web of life, connect more deeply to the Divine in ourselves, enable our own inner work of healing, and discern our call to move into the world as elders who are prepared to act in solidarity with the poor and the poor Earth.

Dream Work

A Dream is a House

A dream is a house you enter
when all is still,
and the day's fever is hushed.
In the silence you ascend
the stairs fashioned of your
bones,
to the attic
where memory is stored,
and hope is boxed
in Grandmother's trunk.
Slowly, one by one,
you lift lids
in fear
and watch images fly up
taking shape in the dusty air.

There you are in the stories
they create,
trying vainly to change
the past or shape a future
as unsubstantial as air.
Useless activity
and frustration's sweat
wake you,
into reality illumined
by the dream.

Or you enter dream's house,
and descend
into basement damp and fear.
In dark labyrinths,
you are pursued
through corridors of dread.

How is this house so large,
this basement so filled
with spaces
that open into worlds?
You enter, only to exit
into a universe of unnamed
enemies
who pursue you
for no reason
and without end.

Waking, you remember
the house vaguely,
and the memory
of dread
pursues you into day
as the dreams works you
while you work it.

When we are living a life that is too small or is not our own life, dreams present us with images to clothe and make visible the movements, conflicts, desires, interactions, and developments of the unconscious. As Robert Johnson writes: "Dreaming and imagination have a special ability in common: their power to convert the invisible forms of the unconscious into images that are perceptible to the conscious mind." [5] Dreams make the soul visible and they present to the ego the soul gift which we are to embody to the world.

Dreams are meant not for the ego itself, but so that ego can function more effectively as the agent of soul. All the energies and all the many inner selves presented to us in dream come from the one Source and can be traced back to it. In scripture, God often uses dreams to call people or to give guidance. Dream work, therefore, is an important tool for elders who wish to get a heart of wisdom.

We work with our own dreams and also become aware of our unconscious as it manifests itself in fantasies, sudden bursts of emotion, or automatic thoughts. "Our isolation from the unconscious is synonymous with our isolation from our souls, from the life of the spirit. It results in the loss of our religious life, for it is in the unconscious that we find our individual conception of God." [6]

Perhaps isolation from our unconscious is one reason that so many elders never do the inner work of this stage of life. Certainly, dream work will help us connect to the creative Source that keeps us alive to ourselves, to God, to creation, and to other people.

There are many ways to do dream work, and elders will find methods that fit their individual needs and inclinations, but the beginning of each method is writing the dream in the first person. A helpful second step is to rewrite the dream in what I have learned from Animas Valley Institute to call an "of me" telling. In this writing, each person, animal, object, building is appended with the words "of me." "I am in the forest *of me*, where I meet the white-tailed deer *of me*. She has a beautiful face *of me* and allows me to touch me and look into the face *of me*."

After writing our dream in these two ways, we could use Robert Johnson's four steps for dream work as outlined in his book *Inner Work*. Another method might be to follow Jill Mellick's approach in which creative expressions are used to work the dream and to let the dream work you. [7]

Working with dreams in a group often gives an intentionality that may be lacking otherwise, but it is essential for elders who do so to cultivate an atmosphere of respect, curiosity, attentiveness, and non-judgment. It is also important to establish a clear framework for the group, including such issues as confidentiality, group membership, taking turns, timing, and freedom to speak or be silent. It is also important to cloak the group in ritual.

"If the energy shows up in a dream image, then it already exists in the psyche of the dreamer. The invisible has been rendered visible. The task of consciousness is to begin to consider this energy, to weigh its presence and to incorporate it into the conduct of daily life." [8] Those of us who want to be conscious in elderhood enter these depths and return with gifts to deepen our connection to soul and spirit, and to anchor us more fully in our own lives.

Art

> There is a river whose streams
> make glad the city of God,
> the holy habitation of the Most High. [9]
> Psalm 46:4

The image of a river is a symbol for me of both creativity *and* spirituality. The river of spirituality is the stream of divine life that flows through everything, gives life to everything, and makes glad the city of God. The river of creativity is the source of the spontaneity and mystery which give birth to the Universe—the river which flows in every creative act of the soul—whether in art-making, in work, in relationships, in gardening, in building a home, or in the tasks of daily life.

Spirituality and creativity are the same river. In making art and in other spiritual practices, we go down to the river. There we immerse ourselves in the flow of image, symbol, and metaphor which are the language of both creativity and spirituality.

Making art is a *spiritual* process. The contemplation of art is *meditation*. Both are spiritual practices which engage us with the Divine. Through both spirituality and creativity, we discover the mystery of the Three in One, the mystery of our creation in God's image, the mystery of the incarnation of God in Jesus, in others and in us, and the mystery of the realm of God that is both within us and in the world.

Engaging in a spiritual discipline is a *creative* process. When we engage with the Divine through meditation, prayer, or mindfulness, we are doing our soul work and we are being created anew. Our theology and faith are being created anew. When we engage with the divine through community, or through acts of compassion, or participation in the great work of the realm of God, our understanding of the issues and needs of the world is made new, along with the particularities of *our* call to "do justice, and to love kindness, and to walk humbly with [our] God." [10]

My Inner Elder

After a dream about an old woman who said to me, "We have to talk," I drew this sketch. In the drawing, I see lines of wisdom and laughter. This woman is the elder I want to become.

Art is a life-giving spiritual practice at any stage of life, and one which elders can engage with joy because we have largely gotten over the notion that we have to be artists. Instead, we recognize that it is the *process* of making art which engages soul and spirit. It is the images, not the skill with which they are portrayed, that reveal new understandings.

Exercises for Soul and Spirit

Coming to the Quiet

1. On the breath
   Sit quietly and become aware of your breath as it passes in through your nostrils and out through your mouth.
   Keep your focus on those two spots, feeling the coolness as you inhale through your nose.
   Feel the warmth as it passes out through your mouth.
   Continue in this awareness as long as it engages you.
   If your attention wanders, simply return your focus.

2. Through body awareness
   Sit quietly and become aware of your breath.
   Move your awareness to your body.
   Beginning at the top of your head notice the sensations
   you are feeling. Don't name them, just notice them.
   Move your awareness to your neck...your shoulders...
   your arms...your hands...your chest...your back...
   your buttocks...your thighs...your lower legs and feet.
   Continue moving your awareness around your body in this
   way...

3. The Jesus prayer
   Sit quietly and become aware of your breath.
   As you inhale, say in your mind "Lord Jesus Christ."
   As you exhale, say the words, "Have mercy on me."

Meditation
The Waterfall
Use all your senses to imagine yourself walking through a
forest. Deep in the forest, you come upon a stream and you
follow it toward its source—a place where water pours
from a cliff high above you and forms a beautiful rocky
pool where the water is still and deep. You kneel and drink
from the pool and feel the cool water slaking your thirst.
You know that this is life-giving water. The pool is inviting
and so you enter it and feel the coolness of the water on
your body, washing you clean.
You stand under the spray from the falls and the water
seems to be flowing through your body, cleansing your
heart and mind of all the psychic and emotional debris of a
life-time, pouring through the cells of your body and
washing it all away. You rest awhile in the awareness of your
healing and your beauty. You give thanks to God.

Movement
1. Put on music.
   Move as you might when your joints are stiff.
   How does your body feel?
   What emotions are you feeling?
   Stretch and then move freely.

What emotions are you feeling now?

2. Move as you have moved through the stages of life:
   Move on all fours. Really look at the world from
   this level. Move on two legs. Notice the differences in
   how you see things.
   Move as you might with a cane.

3. Put on your favourite music and dance.
   Notice your body and your emotions.

4. Go for a prayer walk, tuning your breath to your steps
   and the words of a mantra.
   > e.g. If your breath seems to have three beats,
   > breathe in to *Breathe in me* and breathe out to
   > *breath of God* or some other expression of three
   > syllables, and take three steps for each
   > inhalation and each exhalation.

   Keep your awareness on your breath and body, and allow
   the mantra to fill your mind.

5. Dance
   > the baby of you,
   > the wobbly toddler of you,
   > the playful child of you,
   > the teenager of you,
   > the responsible adult of you,
   > the parent of you,
   > the mid-life crisis of you,
   > and finally, dance in slow-motion, the elder of you.

6. Focus on a particular part of your body.
   Move it in the way it wants to move.
   Notice what feelings or memories this movement stirs,
   and allow them to pass through and out of your body.

7. If you are working with a particular emotion, imagine an
   animal which seems connected to that feeling.
   Move like that animal.
   Make the vocalizations of that animal.
   Notice what happens in your body.

Dream Work

1. Write your dream in the present tense from the point of view of who you are in the dream.
   Next, write the "of me" version. Every time the word I comes up, write instead, "the ego of me." For every character, animal, and object in the dream, add of me.
   > e.g. "The ego of me is walking down the street of me and enters the house of me, where the windows of me are all shuttered.

2. Cluster:
   Select two or three words or images that jump out at you from your dream.
   Cluster these by writing one of the words in the middle of a page and drawing a circle around it. Let your mind make free associations with that word adding an arrow and circle with the next word, then the next, then the next and so on. When that line of association dries up, go back to the centre word and begin another line of associated words or images. When you have finished, read over your cluster and write a twelve word poem or statement that synthesizes your insights.

3. Gallery:
   Imagine a dream image as the only piece in an art gallery. Stand before it and imagine the image as a piece of art. What medium is it done in?
   What do you think the artist intended?

4. Draw a mandala of a dream
   Draw a large circle on a page. As you remember the dream, doodle inside the circle. Connect and colour the images.
   or
   Divide the circle into quadrants. In one, draw the energy of the dream. In another, draw the images of the dream. In the third, draw the feelings.
   In the fourth, use colour and shapes to muse on the meaning of the dream.
   or
   Fill the circle with geometrical shapes. Shade and colour these as you are drawn to do.

5. Move as an animal in your dream.

6. Cluster your associations with dream characters or images.

7. Take your dream out on the land.
   Carry the images and feelings of a dream into nature.
   As you walk notice what draws you.
   Converse with that being of nature about your dream.

8. Dialogue with people or images from your dream.
   Imagine yourself sitting with a person or image
   from your dream. Engage the other in dialogue.
   Write your name: then ask a question of or make a
   statement to the dream image.
   Write its name and then its response.
   Continue the dialogue in this way.

Art
   1. Witness Writing
      Respond to a work of art using the four steps of witness
      writing as described by Pat Allen. [11]
      1. Describe the images in the work of art.
      2. Journal your emotional response to each image.
      3. Invite each image to speak and record the dialogue.
      4. Offer your gratitude

   2. Collage
      Create a life collage.
      For each decade of your life, gather pictures and
      words or phrases which represent the significant
      events, people, and turning points of that stage of your life.
      Arrange them on a sheet of Bristol board in a design and
      with colours that speak to you.
      Glue them to the board using acrylic medium.
      Allow the images to speak to you through witness writing.

   3. In a meditative way, consider the following art pieces or
      choose some pieces from a book or go to a gallery.
      Consider how the images which you encounter are speaking
      to you in your elderhood.

Tree of Life

What is the state of the tree of your life?

Into
the
Big
Water

Into what bigger life do you sense your life is flowing?

Ancient Stones

Broken Down
Walls

What has broken down in elderhood? What has aged in beauty?

56

The Sacred Mountain

What is the sacred mountain that you are seeking on this journey?

4. Water Colour

Prepare water colour paper by taping it to a board or piece of Plexiglas. Choose two or three colours that speak to you. Wash the colours onto the page with lots of water. Lift the board and tilt it to allow the colours to run together and create shapes and designs. Use witness writing.

5. Doodling

Close your eyes and doodle on a page with a coloured pencil, crayon, or pastel or marker.

Open your eyes and look for images and designs in the doodles. Feel free to rotate the page 90 or 180 degrees. Colour the designs and images as you feel called to.

Use witness writing to allow the images to speak to you.

6. Drawing

i) Draw a sketch of your inner elder.

ii) After walking in nature, draw sketches of trees, rocks, or creatures who spoke to you. Allow these to continue speaking through witness writing.

Notes:

Chapter Six

The Tree in Winter: *Facing Debility and Death*

The Dark Continent

This is the place that has been coming to me
forever—death—the country of my citizenship,
the land where all come and none escape.
It has been in me since birth,
hidden in the geography of past demands,
and future dreams. Now it reveals itself
through the slippage of land, the shifting
of rivers, and the swelling of mountains.
It is in me as surely I am alive,
a strange, dark continent, the final frontier
whose contours, now acknowledged in body and
being must be explored in soul and psyche.

My passport is stamped for entry.
The border beckons, but I am not ready
to cross on foot. Instead, I circle aloft,
do aerial reconnaissance, and take photographs
from afar. I see through the viewfinder dimly.
Confused images develop in my mind, a shadowed valley,
a certain black river, an impenetrable forest whose canopy
admits no light. This is the *dark* continent,
and I am afraid. But still, I desire to see.
I will travel there someday and I would not go
unprepared.

Death is always within, a reality which we manage to ignore for most of our lives. As we age, changes in our bodies begin to reveal the hidden continent waiting to be entered. As we age, debility and death become our teachers, instructing us about energy, about making life-giving choices, about asking questions, and about death in its universal domain. When we face our mortality in the midst of life not just at its end, death informs our wisdom, creates a safe place to die, and wakes us up to life.

When we actively ponder death, we discover that we have more energy, and that our energy is moving in different ways. This new form of energy, according to Zalman Schachter-Shalomi, is *thanatos*, the death instinct, which is the psyche's companion to libido. [12] As in our youth libido leads us to continue our DNA through reproduction, so as we age *thanatos* also urges us to generativity of a different sort. As we age, this energy is surging within us as the urge to leave a legacy—to pass on our seeds as flowers and our flowers as fruit.

When we live from this energy, we become more creative and less afraid. We become more compassionate and less judgmental. We become more silent and, at the same time, less willing to swallow our own truth. We become more gracious but also more assertive. Schachter-Shalomi helps us to understand this process when he writes: "When we de-repress the fear of death, we reclaim the energy that has gone into denial." [13] When we learn to accept death as a friend, we have more energy for life.

Death sends poets, nature, and scripture as tutorial assistants who teach us the necessity of making life-giving choices in the face of death. Powerful images open us to the limited number of our days, and the certainty of our dying frees us from lives that are too small and from all that is trifling and trite. We learn to

inhabit our lives and to be fully present to those who are closest to us. We know what is important to us in the final years of our lives and we make choices to spend our time on the things we value and with the people we love.

The wise heart that death awakens in us has a radical sense of the oneness of the whole Universe, and at the same time, a sense of wonder and gratitude for the diversity and beauty of each individual part. We are grateful for who we are and content to be ourselves.

Death Teaches about Life

We learn to be present in each moment, to live with compassion and gratitude for self and others, and to walk gently on the Earth. These choices lead to life and they come from a wise heart that has faced its own death.

As we age, we also learn that death is not merely personal. At stake is "what happens to our own and other species, to the legacy of our ancestors, to unborn generations, and to the living body of Earth." [14] As we become more aware of our own death, we become infinitely more sensitive to the deaths of wet lands, of wood lots, of ivory billed woodpeckers, and five-lined skinks. With clarity, anger, and sadness, we see the threat to all creation and resolve to do something about it.

As we become more aware of our own death, we are infinitely more aware of the deaths of children in refugee camps and of innocent bystanders in suicide car-bombings. Each death diminishes us and the tolling bell rings with great insistency. Our sadness drives us to prayer and to involvement in activities that do justice and make peace.

In elderhood, death teaches us to care deeply for all creation and for the least and the lost of our world. We become more aware of the world that we are bequeathing to our grandchildren, and are moved to the action which arises from a wise heart.

Some Exercises for Facing Debility and Death

1. Make a List
    List every fear you have about sickness and death.
    Write these fears with marker on rocks.
    Create a ceremony in which you speak these fears to a
    trusted loved one and then throw the rocks into a lake or
    river.

2. Lessons Learned from Illness
    Journal about what you have learned from ill-health that
    you could not have learned in any other way.
    Reflect on how you are or are not living this wisdom.
    Give thanks for what you have learned.

3. Seeing your Death
    Take a few deep breaths and settle into your chair...
    Feel the chair or floor holding you up....
    You do not have to hold yourself up. You are held...
    You are safe... Underneath you are the everlasting arms...
    Imagine yourself walking into your physician's office to
    receive news about recent tests...
    Who do you have with you?
    How are you feeling as you wait?
    The doctor tells you that you only have a few months to
    live...
    Notice your feelings, thoughts, and body responses...
    How do you want to live these last months of your life?
    Imagine yourself doing so...
    Now death is very near...where are you? Who is with you?
    What are you feeling?
    What do you say to those gathered around?
    Imagine yourself leaving your body...
    See your spirit moving into the presence of God...
    Rest for a time in the awareness of that presence...
    When you are ready, open your eyes...
    Respond to your experience with writing or art.

4. Plan Your Own Funeral or Memorial Service.
    What music do you want played?
    What readings would you like read?

What stories would you like told about your life?
Whom would you like to speak?

5. Important Conversations
    Have a conversation with your closest relatives about
    what kind of care you want at the end of your life.
    Make a living will.

6. What Death is Teaching Me About Life
    Make a list of what death is teaching you about life.
    Have a conversation with a trusted friend or family
    member about your learnings.

7. Guided Meditation: Meeting God
    Imagine that you are leaving your body and entering the
    eternal presence of God.
    Have a conversation with God about eternity.
    God tells you that it is not time, but gives you a gift to
    take back with you.
    What is that gift?
    Draw, sculpt, or write a poem about that gift.
    Dialogue with the image.

8. Respond to the following images.
    What do they say to you about your experience of life
    in elderhood?

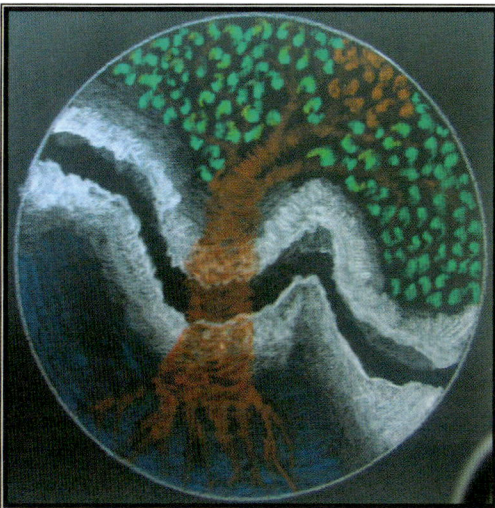

Rooted Across the Ruptures of Age

Juggling Loss and Loneliness

Autumn Patterns

9. "The Dark Continent"
   Meditatively read the poem that begins this chapter.
   First Reading: What images, words, or phrases speak to
        me?
   Second Reading: How is this poem speaking to my life
        today? Where does it connect with my
        present experience?
   Third Reading: Where do I hear the voice of God in this
        poem? How is God speaking to me or
        calling to me?

10. "Words I Hope Will Be Spoken at My Death"
    Read this poem which is found on page 61.
    Think about what words you want spoken at your death.
    Write a poem that speaks these words.

11. Design your Tombstone
    Where do you want to be buried?
    What kind of stone do you want? What shape?
    What words do you want written on it?
    What images?
    What flowers or shrubs do you want planted around it?

12. "When Death Comes"
    Read Mary Oliver's poem by this name in *New and Selected Poems: Volume One.* [15]
    What images speak to you?
    Use oil pastels to draw your own images of death.
    What do you want to be able to say about your life?
    How do you want to face your death?

13. Praying with Play Doh
    Quiet yourself on your breath and follow it inside to the sacred place where the Holy resides within you.
    Without thinking too much about it, let your hand choose a colour of Play Doh.
    With your eyes closed, speak to God about your death.
    As you pray, allow your hands to work with the Play Doh.
    When your conversation is finished, open your eyes and see what your hands have created.
    Use witness writing to let it speak to you.

Notes:

Chapter Seven
Like the Trees: *Doing Everything with Soul*

Of all beings, most blessed
are those with the knack
of being who they are.
The birch,
the hemlock,
the cedar,
the maple—
none tries to sprout legs
or grow wings.
They only shine
with the perfect radiance of being
tree.

Being and Doing

In all of life, we seek to hold the tension between being and doing and we do so with varying degrees of success. However, we live in a society which does not hold *being* in very high esteem, and as a result, we often live the first half of our lives by a code which equates busyness with success. As we age, first retirement and then illness and frailty make a necessity of what seemed like a pleasant spiritual option when we were younger. But we do well to learn the secret of balancing being and doing long before life makes it a necessity, for this balance is a sign of the awakening of a wise heart.

For me, *doing* is all those things by which the ego measures itself as it seeks to create a life and to direct that life toward the goals that denote success to the ego. In our materialistic, achievement-oriented culture, this usually means the accumulation of things and success in one's career.

Being, on the other hand, is all the ways that soul seeks to give its gifts to the world and to surrender to Spirit and to the meaning and purpose that are greater than personality and more lasting than success. It is bringing the wholeness of who one is into every facet of one's life. It is accepting who others are with joy and gratitude.

My ego has much invested in my role as an ordained minister, in my image as a deeply spiritual person, in my role as the good sister who helps to keep the family together, and in being physically, emotionally, *and* psychologically adventurous. Being successful in these is the way that I have shaped my personality, developed self-esteem, and created a life of purpose and meaning for myself.

By and large, at this stage of my life, my ego is healthy. Through the grace of God, I have been able in recent years to become aware of times when I am in danger of thinking that role and image are the true substance of who I am. Although my heart is not always totally convinced, my head knows that because I fail sometimes it does not mean that I *am* a failure. My head knows that because I am spiritually, emotionally and psychologically fairly healthy, this does not make me a better human being than those who are not.

As we age, ego is being called to let go even of this healthy sense of who we are. Like Abraham, called by God to sacrifice the son who was God's promise and gift, we are called to surrender ego to soul because although ego has been able to create a good life, we are not what we do. We are not the role. We are not the image. None of these will last beyond death. Probably, none of these will even survive our aging, and we are being called to invest our self in that which will last forever.

> **Everything with Soul**
>
> Being
> is not idleness,
> but the art
> of doing everything
> with soul.

What we learn in the early stages of elderhood is not that we must give up doing in order to be, but rather that we must learn more fully how to hold the tension between the two and become more soulful in our doing. Any division that still exists between doing and being will be healed through what Parker Palmer calls "rejoining soul and role." [1]

For me, this will mean becoming increasingly aware of when I disappear into my roles by trying to make peace in the family even when there is no peace or by taking care of others even when it means neglecting me. It means becoming increasingly aware of those times when my fear of failure and my need to be liked lead to not speaking my truth, not sharing the latest biblical and theological scholarship, or avoiding conflict by not raising difficult issues of mission and faithfulness in my congregation.

Becoming conscious in elderhood and thereby developing a wise heart means keeping vigilant in our awareness that life is too short to allow ego to have the field to itself. Elderhood is the time of being—the time of soul. Ego, however, puts up a good fight.

Through our inner critics who ask what our worth will be if we do not have work or success by which to measure ourselves, ego resists letting go. Ego, it seems, would rather have us ground our self-worth in falsehood than surrender to soul! Ego can also use pride in how far we have come and how much healing has already happened to try and persuade us that we are okay as we are, and that its death is not necessary.

Even in elderhood we are sometimes in danger of being subsumed or subverted by image or by our need to succeed in our roles, and it is difficult to maintain consciousness about the balance of being and doing.

One strategy that awakens a wise heart is to imagine our lifeless body decaying in the ground. It is amazing how little someone else's approval or a failed project really matter when we remember that we are going to die anyway. Another strategy that cultivates wisdom is to notice ego's voice and choose not to indulge it, but rather to choose partnership with soul instead.

Time to Play

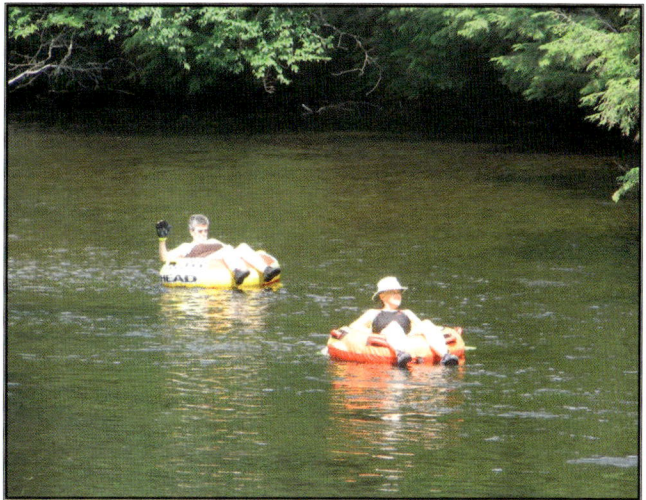

Awe and Wonder

Age Wildly
Go wild gradually. Acre by acre
let go of tidy gardens,
trimmed hedges and straight rows.
Release them to the rank growth
of delight,
and awe,
and wonder.
Let balsam and pine
break down stone walls,
disorder the skyline, and
join heaven and earth
in the dark heart of your longing.
Let wild geese
teach the southward instinct
and the sure return.
Let cycling seasons
teach trust in birthing,
in living and dying,
and in life's certain renewal.
Go wild gradually—
into a fierce freedom.

As we become conscious elders, we learn to balance being and doing and to live more fully in partnership with soul; we recover the awe and wonder of childhood. We find ourselves filled with praise and gratitude for a Universe full of enduring wonders far beyond our imagining. We learn again to delight in nature and in life itself.

In adolescence we are filled with youthful idealism, but life seems to take the bloom off the rose. As we age, we see more of life's misery and pain. Horror threatens to overwhelm beauty; the experience of inexplicable suffering calls our faith into doubt.

As we move into elderhood, those who become conscious are filled anew with a sense of wonder. Sunlight on the snow, a violet blooming in a window, and the softness of a baby's skin have the power to fill us with joy. Once again we are awash with wonder.

Awe and delight arise from a wise heart which knows that all creation is sacred, that matter is imbued with spirit, and that bodies are the locus of our relationship with the Divine. This wise heart teaches us appreciation of diversity and respect for all things in the web of life. We become filled with wonder at the complexity of life and at the uniqueness of every being, and a key principle of our ethic becomes the praise, protection, and preservation of all life.

The wise heart that awakens from awe also confronts the myth of scarcity and leads to a belief in life's abundance. We learn that justice means that everyone has access to enough resources for a good quality of life and that "physical well-being and spiritual fulfilment are most readily attainable through a path of moderation and the avoidance of extremes in consumption." [2] Out of a renewed sense of awe and wonder, those who become conscious in elderhood awaken into a wise heart which has learned to live simply on the earth, to confront patterns of human greed, and to create conditions in which all may live lives of health, well-being and happiness.

Some Exercises for Doing Everything with Soul

1. Breath Prayer

   Sit in a chair or on the floor with your spine straight.
   Focus your attention on the end of your nose where your breath enters your body...
   Feel the coolness as the air enters your nostrils...
   Follow your breath down into your lungs...
   Notice as it expands your belly then your chest...
   Exhale through your mouth...
   Notice the warmth on the roof of your mouth and on your lips...Continue holding your awareness on your breath, letting your body breathe itself...

2. Being and Doing: A Journal Exercise

   Journal about the difference between being and doing in your life. For example:
   What did you busy yourself doing? Why?
   What are you busy with now?
   How are you doing things differently?
   Are the reasons you do things different than they once were?
   Are you comfortable doing nothing? Why or why not?

3. Being and Doing: A Clustering Exercise
   Cluster the word "being." Write a haiku based on the key
   ideas in your cluster. Do the same for the word "doing."
      In English, a haiku is a three line poem.
      Line 1: 5 syllables
      Line 2: 7 syllables
      Line 3: 5 syllables
         for example:

                    Falling into death
                  I rise to the Universe:
                    life in its fullness.

                    Sailing into age
                  still full-rigged, I dare the seas
                    of my elderhood.

4. Being and Doing: A Conversation with Sacred Other
   Go out into nature and spend some time with something in
   nature that captures your attention.
   Get to know it with all your senses.
   Introduce yourself and ask this being about itself.
   Have a conversation about being and doing.

5. An Art Exercise with your Inner Child
   Sit comfortably with crayons, markers, or pastels.
   Quiet yourself through awareness of your breath...
   Close your eyes and see or feel a child playing near you...
   Notice everything about him or her...hair colour, clothing,
   height, posture...What game is he or she playing?
   He or she invites you to play and you join in...
   What are you feeling?
   Now imagine the two of you sitting on the ground or
   floor...Let the child draw a picture for you using your non-
   dominant hand. Have a conversation with the child about
   play...Thank the child for this time together.

6. A Day Retreat
   Plan and make a day retreat for yourself in which you spend
   time in solitude doing things that you love.

7. A Play Date with Your Inner Child
   Remember some of the things you loved to do as a child.
   Take your inner child out to play.

8. A Journal Exercise about Childhood
   Journal about yourself as a child.
   What did you love to do?
   What were your dreams?
   Which of these dreams might you incorporate into your life now?

9. A Lament
   Have some clay or Play Doh in front of you.
   Quiet yourself in a way that is comfortable for you.
   Work the clay in your hands as you:
   Invoke God's presence...
   Cry out in lament for all the energy and time you spent on what did not truly satisfy...
   Ask for help...
   Express your trust in God...
   Make a vow...

10. A Prayer of Gratitude
    Create a prayer of gratitude for the ways your soul was able to express itself in your work and other activities. Dance that gratitude to your favourite music.

11. Read the Elder Tale: "The Builder's Dream"
    How does this speak to you about recovering awe, wonder and innocence as you age?

12. The Wonder of Nature
    Go out on a clear night away from city lights. Take a lawn chair so you can sit and look at the stars. Notice your thoughts and feelings.
    Get up early and go to a place where you can watch the sunrise. Gather the light into your eyes, into your mouth and into your whole body. Feel the joy of being filled with light.

13. Respond to the following images.

The Balance of Being and Doing

What is the still point that balances being and doing for you?

What practices hold you in that stillness?

What does it mean to you to be a feather on the breath of God?

Be Still and Know

What is your inner place of stillness where you know
that who you are is not grounded in what you do?
How do you access that place?
What do you feel when you are there?
How can you stay in that place despite whatever else is
going on in your life?

Notes:

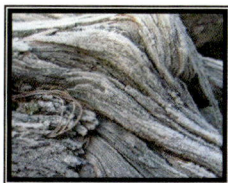

Chapter Eight
Fallen Leaves: *Coming to Terms with our Lives*

As we grow through the various stages of our lives, we are constantly coming to terms with who we are, how we act in our intimate relationships, what we are making of our lives, how we are using or squandering our gifts, where we are seeking meaning and purpose, and what is the nature of our faithfulness to our ultimate values. In old age, this task takes on urgency and poignancy as we turn toward home, and so, before we release our lives into the Great Mystery, we seek the wise heart that is at peace with what our lives have been.

Life Review

You go down into the basement
      into memory.
Down into dirt
      and regret.
Into the secret past,
    found in pocketed stones,
    kept coins,
    and scraps of paper.
You separate memories
    into white and colours,
    hot and cold:
    the loads of your life,
    washed with tears,
    rinsed with compassion,
    dried in the heat of loss.
Then you come upstairs
      into cleanliness,
into refreshment
    and clarity,
ready
    for a new history,
    wearing the old like a clean shirt.

In old age, the laundry of our experience needs washing. Treasures crave being found in the pockets of memory; wounds of the past yearn to be cleansed, and lost parts of our selves long to be recovered. We sink down into our minds and begin the task of laundering our memories in order to come to terms with our successes and failures, our joys and sorrows, our regrets and unfinished business.

There are, however, two kinds of thinking. There is thinking that is *escape*, and there is thinking that is *engagement*. The first is deadening, while the second is enlivening and growth-filled. We escape into the mind when we spend time in our memory— regretting the past, longing for what is no more, or wounded by what was in such a way that we are prevented from living in the present moment.

We engage with memory when our reflection on experience is a critique of ideas and concepts that helps us to clarify our own thinking. We engage with our memory when reflection and critique lead to transformation in the moment. Such engagement both comes from and awakens a wise heart.

When we become conscious in elderhood, we drop into memory for the purpose of transformation. We visit old places so that we can see new vistas and move into deeper understanding of ourselves and the world. We travel through time and memory in order to synthesize our life experience into a story which holds together all the disparate elements of our lives in an integrated whole and in doing so, we "clarify and increase what we are." [1]

Memory's Path

Out of our wrestling with memory, we walk memory's path and sift all our life experience, perceptions, skills, and relationships and begin to note in them patterns, not only of our own making but of the Divine. Through the wisdom that is awakened by coming to terms with our lives, we are able to rise above despair at what our lives have and have not been into a sense of our oneness with all interrelated beings. We rise also into communion with the Spirit of the Universe.

Three Processes for Coming to Terms with our Lives

Spiritual Intelligence

Richard Wolman's discussion of spiritual intelligence provides insight about the work of coming to terms with our lives in elderhood. He offers a "definition of intelligence, including spiritual intelligence, that adheres to the following sequence: *noticing, knowing, understanding, emotional satisfaction/action.*" [2]

In elderhood, we notice particular life events in an intentional or random way and hold them up to the light of our past experience and internal standards. We may feel guilt, or regret, or a sense of accomplishment, and these feelings help us to know the meaning of this event in the arc of our life experience. Finally, we choose a course of action suitable to the place of this event in our inner lexicon. We may choose, for example, to make amends for a wrong we have done, to forgive someone who hurt us, to give thanks for our blessings, to develop a neglected gift or talent, or to hold our hurt in the healing light of Divine Love.

Through this process, we awaken into a heart of wisdom—the integration of body, mind and spirit—sense, memory, and meaning—for the purpose of finding ultimate values and meanings in our experience. We seek to embody those values and meanings in our way of being and doing in the elderhood. By telling the truth, but also by telling stories, we put our lives into perspective so that we are at peace.

After ten years of ill-health, my father died at age sixty. I was twenty-one years old. Ever since, I have felt cheated of the experience of getting to know my father as adult to adult. I did not know much about him as a person and he never had the opportunity to see the woman I have become and what I have made of my life. This loss has always been a source of regret and of speculation.

One day, when I was going through a box of old photographs, I found a picture that dad had taken in the winter of 1940 when he was thirty years old and doing a locum filling in for a physician in Clinton, Ontario. On the back of the photograph, he had written a description of when and where he had taken the picture and the settings he had used on the camera. Tears came to my eyes as I thought of all the things I never knew about dad and all I had missed because of his early death. That strong emotion made me realize that I still had work to do on this issue and I wrote the following poem as a way of coming to terms with the loss.

Snow Drift, Clinton
Snow drift, Clinton,
Easter Sunday, 1940
f22, 1/25 sec, bright.

These words and figures
in my father's hand
let loose hot tears.

In the photograph,
telephone poles stand cruciform
in a white sky.
Shadows of trees branch blackly
on a wasteland of snow.
Wire-high drifts
bisect light above,
and dark beneath.
Shadows fade to the horizon.

All is artfully composed:
dark and light,
death and life,
Easter, 1940.

The writing reveals
a meticulous mind,
a scientific skill; the photograph
portrays an artist's soul.

Was he so complex, my father,
divided in mind and heart?
Or are my own conflicted feelings
the source
of these hot tears?

Lament

Lament is a spiritual practice which may help us come to terms with our lives and so get a heart of wisdom as we age. As it applies to the task of coming to terms with our lives in elderhood, lament is the work of seeing our lives clearly, grieving our wrongs of commission and omission, and taking appropriate action to put things right. In this spiritual practice, we bring the "sorrowful mysteries" of our lives before God in such a way that we can find healing and forgiveness. [3] We dare to see ourselves clearly and to allow our seeing to penetrate our numbness and forgetting. We name our wounds and our wrongs, and let our hearts be pierced by this naming so that we truly feel our grief, sorrow, and regret.

Lament in this context may take the form of ritual as we find it in scripture. In the Psalms, the structure of lament includes: a cry to God, a candid description of the situation, a prayer for help and deliverance, the reasons why God should help, a vow of praise or action to be fulfilled when the prayer is heard, and finally, our grateful praise to God.

We begin our lament by naming God as the One in whose love we can find the courage to face ourselves. With as much candour and honesty as we can muster, we then name our faults and failings and all the ways we have separated ourselves from God, from others, and from our truest self. We cry out to God from the depths of our pain and grief, seeking God's forgiveness and healing. We name our confidence in God as the One who is steadfast in love and mercy. We offer up actions which will put things right, and finally, we praise the Holy One from a place of gratitude and joy. Such lament is a powerful practice for coming to terms with our lives in elderhood, and truthfully, in any time of our lives, and it awakens us to a heart of wisdom.

Critical Reflection

Another practice which helps us elders in the task of coming to terms with our lives is critical reflection. As I age, it seems that I reflect on everything through the lens of dying and rising—the dying and rising of Jesus Christ and the dying and rising which are evident in the whole Universe. Everywhere, there are forces that lead to life and those that lead to death, those that are of God and those that are not. The forces that lead to death—in me, in others and in the world—are the forces I struggle against. The forces of life are the ones that I seek to enhance, cooperate with, and live into.

In the task of coming to terms with our lives, we reflect on our experience through this lens of death and life. The forces that lead to death might be things like fear, perfectionism, pride, or self-loathing, and so the practice of critical thinking about our lives becomes one of "uncovering…hidden drives [and] distorted self-images"—both the grandiose and the devaluing which underlie our actions and relationships. [4] This practice of reflection can uncover what has been repressed in our Shadow, and help us to withdraw from others our projections of both the good and the bad in our own psyches.

Thus, in elderhood, the practice of critical reflection through the lens of death and resurrection awakens a wise heart which can hold the tension between the beautiful and the broken in ourselves, and help us navigate our days with greater grace and compassion for ourselves and for others.

Critical reflection through the lens of death and resurrection can help us to come to terms with the choices that we have made earlier in life and are now making in our elderhood. We come to see which choices are healthy for us and enable us "to deal creatively with the problems of [elderhood]—to confront them, withstand them, cope with them, grow from them." [5] Through this reflection, we come to understand the necessity of choices that create a balance of time alone with time spent with others, rote tasks with creativity, work with play, and the needs of others with our own needs. Critical reflection in elderhood, as a way of coming to terms with our lives, awakens a wise heart which is able to hold the tension between these contradictions inherent in old age.

As elders who are striving to be conscious, another area for critical reflection is relationships. "Learning to distinguish between what we can and cannot change, taking responsibility for our actions, and then letting go of the rest" is an essential component of coming to terms with our relationships. [6] We see what has been and is life-giving in our relationships and what has contributed to the deaths of relationships. We see where God has been at work to bring new life in us and in our intimate companions.

Out of this reflection, we see where we have done what we

could and tried to be the best person we could be in the relationship. We recognize our flaws and those of others, and seek to love our Self, the other, *and* the relationship. We see how new life becomes manifest in our higher tolerance for diversity and dissonance, and in a greater ability to speak the truth and to express our needs while also respecting those of others. We recognize that though we have not always succeeded, life has been at work in us and in our intimate relationships.

The methodologies of spiritual intelligence and critical reflection and the ritual of lament are helpful practices in waking up in elderhood and developing the wise heart which enables us to come to terms with our lives.

Some Exercises for Coming to Terms with our Lives

1. A Clustering Exercise
    "Contentment is the desired state of elderhood – to be at peace with what has been, what is, and what will be."
    Cluster the word contentment.
    Write a haiku which captures the most significant insights.

2. Death Lodge
    Imagine that the time of your death is near.
    You retire from the life of your community and go to the Death Lodge.
    Here your friends and relatives will come to greet you.
    This is a last opportunity to say goodbye.
    As you receive each one in turn, you say what you must say now that you are dying.
    Now in the twilight of your life, you love them as never before.
    You make peace.
    You give away everything to them.

3. Marshalling your Strengths: Mining the inner resources of your past.
    Name a difficult or challenging time in your life.
    What did you learn, how did you grow, how were you gifted in unforeseen ways?
    What strengths/resources do have now to meet the challenges of elderhood?
    Draw a shield symbolizing your strengths.

or

Use the imagery from Ephesians 6 of the armour of God:
The resources I have learned from the past are:

> The belt of...
> The breastplate of...
> The shoes of...
> The shield of...
> The helmet of...

4. Letters of Gratitude
   Write letters of gratitude to the people in whom God accompanied you through your life.

5. A Ceremony of Self-Forgiveness
   Think back through the decades of your life.
   In each decade, what are the actions for which you have a hard time forgiving yourself?
   Write these down.
   Create a ceremony for forgiving yourself.

6. Forgiving Others
   In your journal write a letter to a person with whom you have unresolved hurts.
   Pour out your feelings, thoughts, and ideas without censoring them.
   Put yourself in the other person's shoes and write a letter back.
   See the two of you bathed in divine light that melts resentment and allows forgiveness to flow.
   Read the letters over and ask yourself:
   "What insights have I gained?"
   Create a ceremony for releasing the letters.

7. Create a Life Map Collage
   In each decade of your life:
   What were the significant events, experiences, and turning points?
   Who were the people who influenced you for good or ill?
   What did you learn in this stage of life that has carried through into the present?
   Using pictures and words make a collage of your life.

8. Healing Painful Memories.

   In your imagination, begin at your present age and send your mind further and further back into your past...

   Stop when you come to a painful memory...a time of turmoil, a failure, the breakdown of a relationship...

   Allow yourself to experience all the feelings of your younger self...Now let your elder self reach back in time and be with your younger self, offering comfort, support, and encouragement...Visualize an embrace in which your elder self blesses your younger self...Hear the words of your elder self...You will make it through this time...

   You will learn valuable lessons from this experience...Be at peace...All will be well...Feel yourself letting go of this pain...giving thanks for its blessings...making it holy by offering it up...As you let go, notice your breath and become aware of any increased energy, buoyancy, or new courage...Give thanks... Journal.

9. Respond to the following image by asking yourself:

   As I age, what issues that I need to deal with are being reflected in the windows of my soul?

Reflection

Notes:

Chapter Nine
Still Green: Discovering What We Yet May Be

The Unknown

The unknown lies just over the horizon.
It knows delicious secrets,
        future mysteries,
            people gone on or not yet arrived.
It knows the one I yet may be.

The unknown wears maternity clothes,
        spandex pants and baggy tops
        so it can grow,
            become,
                give birth.
Its work is expectancy
        and eating:
            nourishing itself with trust.
Its joy is waiting to see who comes.
The unknown plays solitaire,
        and listens
            for sounds of arrival.
It is an adventure,
        a wrapped gift,
        a path winding out of sight.

In the unknown, I might get lost
        or even die,
but the journey is everything:
            experience
            learning,
            life.

Journeying to the unknown,
I take with me memory and the hope
of what I yet may be.

In the research I did with retired United Church ministers on their experience of elderhood, four out of five participants identified a need and a desire to continue growing in their elderhood—spiritually, emotionally, and intellectually. Most expressed a desire to stay open to changes in the world and in the Church. Some also expressed a desire to keep up with changes in theology, while one was anxious to deepen into traditional teachings in order to hold him fast in the face of change.

When we seek to wake up into elderhood, one facet of wise-hearted consciousness is an understanding that we still desire to and are able to learn—about ourselves, other people, and the world. As those who wish to become conscious in elderhood, we seek to initiate and/or deepen awareness about personal growth issues that we still need to and want to address in our lives.

We think about who we still want to become and what growth will be necessary for that becoming. Along with ritual, dream work, and interaction with nature, we develop or deepen practices of creativity, growing in Christ, and asking good questions. These practices enable us to become what we yet may be.

Creativity

Often, part of what elders seek to fulfil are the creative gifts which were ignored earlier in life, either because they were not valued in our families of origin or because we were too busy making a living and raising our families. Now, in elderhood, there is time for creative pursuits and a desire to develop these lost parts of ourselves.

To be creative is to risk failure and foolishness, but elders, by and large, have moved beyond being afraid to fail or to appear foolish. By facing death, we are no longer as afraid of the little death that is failure—the death of self-esteem. "In the perspective of death it is a privilege to be alive and fail," and having confronted the spectre of death, those of us who become conscious in elderhood find a wise-hearted daring which enables us to explore our creativity. [7] By risking failure and foolishness, we can not only grow into unlived parts of ourselves, but also open the space for new insights about ourselves and the world. Because the energy and joy of creativity are so great, creativity enables us to move toward what we yet may become.

Creativity is an experience sufficient unto itself; nothing needs to be added to it because creativity is full of meaning in itself. Something creative is born from us but it is also born from a power that moves through us. It comes from within us, but also from the Great Mystery, the ground of existence. When we create, it is I, but not I, because sacred otherness is present in what we are doing. When we create, we are deeply connected to God who is the source of creativity, growth, and transformation. Exercising creativity in elderhood is a path to deeper consciousness and a wise heart.

Growing in Christ

As Christians, the process of getting a heart of wisdom is the process of growing "to maturity, to the measure of the full stature of Christ." [8] This process is essential to our faith, and it continues in elderhood. As Christians, growing in Christ is our way of fulfilling Gandhi's advice to become the change we want to see. Christ lived the change he wanted to see in the world, and so we seek to grow into his likeness—to become people of compassion, justice, hospitality, and acceptance.

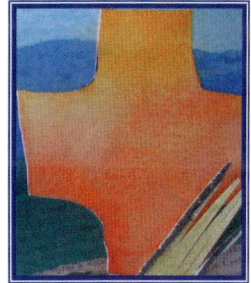

By continuing to grow in Christ, we learn to trust God in the experiences which old age brings to us—the wilderness of grief, the valley of despair, the mountain top of wisdom, the night-time of our body's betrayal, and even death. By continuing to grow in Christ, we live more deeply into the divine life within and increasingly from the compassionate heart of Jesus. We become more attuned to the values of the reign of God and live more naturally in its shalom.

By becoming more and more like Christ, we become conscious in elderhood and learn the wisdom which is as wily as snakes and as gentle as doves. "When the moment calls for fierceness, [we are] very ferocious. And when the moment calls for kindness, [we are] utterly tender. [And in knowing] which moment is which" we awaken into the wisdom of our years. [9] This "wisdom is not sublime metaphysical knowledge, but a skill that helps solve real human problems." [10] We speak the truth with love and act for justice and peace as we bring wisdom and courage into our relationships and into our communities in practical ways.

Good Questions

As we continue to grow, those who are becoming conscious adopt a stance which says, "Question everything." This perspective, which comes from long experience of life's vagaries, pushes us to question our personal lives and assumptions, as well as the assumptions which underlie the culture and the institutions to which we belong. For Christian elders, some of our best questions ask if what we are doing, thinking, and saying is congruent with God's reign, and whether what we are doing helps or hinders us in keeping our identity as Christ's people in the world.

Such questions abound in scripture. "Do you love me?" (John 21:16c) "Who do you say that I am?" (Mark 8:29) "Why do you spend your money for that which is not bread, and your labor for that which does not satisfy?" (Isaiah 55:2) "Whom shall I send, and who will go for us?" (Isaiah 6:8b) "Is this not the fast that I choose: to loose the bonds of injustice, to undo the thongs of the yoke, to let the oppressed go free; and to break every yoke?" (Isaiah 58:6) [11]

Such questions, when focused on our lives in elderhood, help us to see clearly where we need to grow and how we can continue to become more like Christ. Being confronted with these questions from scripture, we begin to ask our own questions. *What is God still calling me to do with my life? Am I spending my limited time and energy on the things and people that are really important to me? What do I really believe at this stage of my life and how does it affect my living and dying?* Answering these questions is the voyage of the wise heart.

Still Sailing Full-rigged

What seas are you sailing as you seek to continue to grow in elderhood?

How is the wind of the Spirit calling and pushing you to become what you yet may be?

Some Practices for Becoming What We Yet May Be

1. Guided Meditation: A Visit to Your Inner Elder
    Quiet yourself with awareness of your breath...
    Notice your breath as it passes in and out through your nostrils...
    Notice how deeply your breath is going into your body...
    Your breath is opening sacred space within you for the Holy One...
    Rest in the awareness of this openness and expectancy...
    Now imagine that you are walking on a path through the woods...
    Imagine that woods with all your senses...What do you see...smell...hear...feel?
    You walk for some time and eventually, in the distance, you see a stone cottage...
    Something in you recognizes this place and knows that someone is waiting there for you...
    You walk up to the door and knock...
    As the door opens, you look into the eyes of your Inner Elder, your fully realized self who is looking at you with boundless love and great joy...
    You are invited in and you ask your Inner Elder a question about an issue or a choice you are facing...
    You wait for an answer in a state of open-hearted trust...
    You receive an answer, either as a symbol, an image, a word, or an inner knowing...
    You speak with your Inner Elder about the knowing you have received...
    As you look again into the eyes of your Inner Elder, you receive a blessing...
    Imagine this blessing unfolding in your daily life...
    You know that you can return to your Inner Elder any time you wish, with any questions or concerns...
    With gratitude, you say goodbye and walk back through the woods, arriving at the place of your departure...
    You return your awareness to that place...
    and when you are ready, you open your eyes...
    Draw your Inner Elder or make a collage of images, pictures, and words that express the wisdom, insight, and blessing you have received.

2. A Cluster Exercise
   Cluster the words "becoming an elder"
   Write a haiku or a 10 word sentence based on the key ideas
   of your clustering.

3. A Visualization of The Elder You Want to Become
   Visualize yourself as the elder you want to become.
   What does an average day look like?
   Where are you giving your energy and time?
   How do you recharge your batteries?
   Where are you living?
   Who are your most important relationships?

4. Lists
   List 10 personal goals you want to attain before you run
   out of time.
   List 10 talents you want to realize.
   Create a plan for realizing them and take the first step.

5. Fire Ceremony
   Create a ceremony in which you write down, lament, then
   ritually burn your fears and doubts, and the self which is
   too small.
   Write your fears and doubts on a piece of paper
   Lament: Invoke God's presence...
                  Cry out all your fears and doubts to God,
                  lamenting the ways in which you have lived a life
                  that is too small...
                  Ask for help...
                  Express your trust in God...
                  Make a vow...
   Ritually burn your fears and doubts
   Offer thanksgiving to God

6. Taking a Dream to God
   Imagine one dream or desire that you would still like to
   fulfill in your life...
   Place this dream in your heart...
   Surround it with love as you hold it there...
   Breathe the Spirit's life and energy into your heart...

With pencil or pen, draw a picture of this dream in your heart.
With that picture before you, do this visualization every day.
Keep track of openings, steps, images, people, and serendipitous happenings that help you on your way toward this dream.

7. Elder Vision Statement
   Write a vision statement for your elder years.
   Have it printed or write it in calligraphy.
   Frame it and keep it where you can see it every day.

8. Imagine that you are with Jesus.
   He turns to you and asks a question.
   What does he ask?
   How do you respond?

9. Make a list of questions that your life is asking of you in elderhood.

10. How is Christ calling you to grow in your elderhood?
    What are your growing edges?

11. Read the following poem in a Lectio Divina format.
    Read it through once aloud and note any words or phrases that speak to you. Take time in silence to ponder them.
    Read it through aloud a second time and note where the poem is speaking to your daily life. Take time in silence to ponder these connections.
    Read the poem aloud a third time, asking yourself: what is God calling me to do? How is God calling me to grow?

    Grace and a Riddle
    Grace has engendered a riddle.
    I hear a knock,
    and open the door,
    but no one is there.
    Who knocked then, and
    what did I hear?
    Why did I answer,
    if no one called?

This present absence,
engendering an enigma,
is a code so strong within
that I respond body and soul.
I want to become wise and so
I can do no other.
There is no answer to be solved,
only a mystery to be lived,
an absent presence
to be sought and savoured,
unseen.

Knock, knock!
Who's there?

I ride this riddle
as on a quest, seeking
an answer to the enigma of self.
First east, then south,
west, then north
to the sun's rising and its setting,
I test my ingenuity
in divining the mystery of me.

I wander through grasses
and wildflowers wanting answers,
longing for prescience and purpose.
The travelled tracks deepen,
cutting the landscape of life,
across and back,
leading nowhere.

Then, out of need,
and beyond hope, a presence.
Coming down the path I made with my wanderings
is grace
engendered by a riddle.

And I grow.

12. Make a list of ten things you would try if it did not sound too crazy.

13. Who Am I Living for Anyway?
    Many of us live our lives trying to please others and don't pay enough attention to our own needs.
    Complete the following statements as a way of discovering how you can more fully embrace your own desires, needs, and joys at this stage of your life.

    I spend most of my time and energy on_____

    The biggest barrier to fulfilling my dreams is _____

    My greatest joy is _____

    My greatest need is _____

    I wish I could _____

    I don't because _____

    When I take care of myself, I _____

    When I put others' needs first, I _____

14. Collage
    Collect images of all the things you want to do before you are no longer able to do them.
    Arrange the images on a piece of poster board and play with arranging them until how they are placed seems right.
    Glue them down using acrylic medium.
    Place this Collage in your worship centre.
    Meditate on it every day.
    Notice yearnings and openings toward the fulfilment of these dreams.
    Put some of them into action.

Notes:

Chapter Ten
The Tree of Life: *Spirituality and Faith*

Issues of faith and spirituality are born of our encounter with life and, in elderhood, out of the proximity of death. The spiritual task for those who wish to become conscious in elderhood is to be alive to the movements of God's story in our stories, to discover the authority and authenticity of our own experience, and to be grounded in our own faith tradition while holding it lightly. This task is not undertaken "as an interesting intellectual exercise, but as an impassioned examination of [our] ultimate values and commitments." [1] It is an active, personal inquiry into our beliefs about meaning and purpose, our place in the universe, about God, Jesus, the soul, and life after death. It is an act of love in which elders can model an open-hearted, curious journey of faith and encourage others to journey in the same manner. It is a way of awakening a wise heart.

Spirituality and Faith

When we dare to engage in this inquiry, those who are becoming conscious often find that out of our life experience we have come to think of God in a new way. The Sunday School God of our youth cannot hold together the questions and doubts that we pushed to the back of our minds earlier in life and which now are arising in the nearness of death. Our new way of thinking, however, does not aim for correct doctrine about God as much as it aims for union with God, and from that union, for action which is concomitant with a God of love. Our thinking at this stage of life seems to arise from a conviction that "it is not, then, so important that 'I believe in God' as it is to align my life with and toward this reality. I must try to discover what it means to live in the reality that is defined by love." [2]

In the course of our living, those who are becoming conscious discover that God is not a being out there, separate from all reality, but is the *ground* of all reality, is even reality itself. God, elders find, is the Breath that gives life and the Spirit who transforms life. When we become conscious, we come to see that "Wisdom (*sophia*) defines the kind of Spirit that God's Spirit is...a persuading, inviting, educing, communicating agency, acting not merely in human interaction but throughout the whole cosmic reality." [3]

Iona Abbey

Those who become conscious have to come to grips with the reality that the Christian understanding of God has been and still is implicated in much oppression and suffering in the world. In this struggle with faith and life, we have to let go of old certainties and former ways of thinking and speaking about God. We have to come to terms with a profound unknowing and, at the same time, learn a trust deeper than any we have yet experienced.

However, when this all is said and done, many find, as Thomas Moore does, that "the presence of God is more real to [us] now than it ever was, and yet it is also emptier of ideas and certainties. [We] feel that [our] notion of God has matured year by year, and yet [we] now know less about God not more. The old paradoxes express God's nature better than any plain statements...God is beyond any image [we] might have and yet requires the best of images. Anything [we] say about God [we] must undo at the very moment [we] say it, and yet [we] don't need to stop talking." [4] When we become conscious, we speak of God with passion and know that what we say is provisional and partial.

Gratitude

①ne thing, however, that is not provisional and partial in the spirituality and faith of conscious elders is gratitude. With more of our lives behind us than ahead of us, we realize with new force how precious and full of gifts life is, and the practice of gratitude will keep us open to that realization. Gratitude awakens us to beauty, to wonder, to love, to ourselves, and to others. Gratitude frees us to love and to accept self and other; it enables us to discover our soul gifts and to give them away as the only fitting response to the Giver. Gratitude awakens a wise heart.

God Sees the Sparrow

Gratitude keeps us connected to others, because through our thankfulness, we recognize our dependence on a myriad of people and on the earth itself. When we offer prayers of gratitude, we recognize that our hard-won independence is necessary, but also illusory. Standing on our own was a vital step in becoming who we are, but at the same time, we have not done it alone. We have been dependent on the love and support of others at every step along the way.

Those who become conscious in elderhood cherish the strong people we become, but also know that we are dependent on farmers, truckers, and grocery clerks, on family and friends, and on sun, rain and earth for our day-to-day needs. We know that we are dependent on people for our emotional needs, and, most of all, on God, for our very being. The spiritual practice of gratitude awakens elders to the wisdom which holds the tension between dependence and independence, and which trusts the Christ in whom all things hold together.

In his letter to the Philippians, St. Paul writes, "in everything by prayer and supplication *with thanksgiving* (italics mine) let your requests be made known to God." [5] Those who are becoming conscious discover that gratitude is not just offered for life's blessings and joys, but is the leaven that enables us to rise above difficulty and sorrow. No matter how busy, down-hearted, or anxious we are, if we "keep the fertile balance of honoring both [our] joy and sorrow", [we are] transformed. [6] The situation may not change, but we are changed. Practising gratitude enables elders, to cultivate the wise heart which holds the tension between joy and sorrow, life and death, intimacy and loss, and which trusts the Christ in whom all things hold together.

The gratitude that wells up in the face of death can teach elders that death, but also life, is at the very heart of the universe, and that both can be trusted. "Prayers of thanksgiving assume beyond a shadow of a doubt that God, who already knows our needs (Mt. 6:8) will meet them." [7]

In the practice of gratitude, as we elders become more aware of and thankful for the synergies and serendipities that have graced our way, we learn that the power of the Universe is both personal and beneficent. Gratitude enables us to acquire the wisdom which holds the tension between doubt and faith, and trusts in the Christ who holds all things together.

My Spirituality and Faith

While acknowledging that everything I know is provisional and partial, I am still seeking understanding and trying to express my faith in a systematic way. I am still doing the work of theology, but now, at this stage of my life, from an ecofeminist perspective which begins with experience.

My lived experience and that of the people to whom I belong and among whom I minister is the experience of a western, middle-class, white, educated, privileged people who, for the most part, have endless possibilities for work, prosperity, and happiness. It is the experience of people who live in a consumer-driven, petrochemical-based society and have unknowingly internalized the ideology of materialism, and who often seek its values to give meaning to life. We uncritically interpret our experience based on the thought patterns of patriarchy—the superiority of spirit over matter and masculine over feminine, the goal of transcending the material world, and the value of pyramidal, personal, exclusive power.

At the same time, my experience and that of the people among whom I belong is one of listening to the plurality of voices from around the world—the voices of the homeless in our city streets, the voices of the exploited workers in the two-thirds world, the voices of the dispossessed in Sudan and Burma. It is the experience of those who are beginning to hear the cries of Earth as it suffers from global warming, loss of bio-diversity, and extinction of species.

Out of this lived-world experience, we see God at work bringing blessing and prosperity—the God of our personal well-being, the source of strength in our troubles, and the connective tissue of community. We see God suffering in the poor and dispossessed and in the degradation of Earth, and we experience God at work in the unsettling of our comfortable lives through the cries of the poor and the poor Earth. We see God at work in wells dug to provide clean water in Mozambique, in Karen refugees sponsored from Burma, and in all acts of justice and peace.

It is in the light of these experiences, that I am seeking to understand who God is. It is these very experiences and the God I see in the midst of them that shape an eco-feminist theology. It is this theology that sustains and guides me as I enter my elder years.

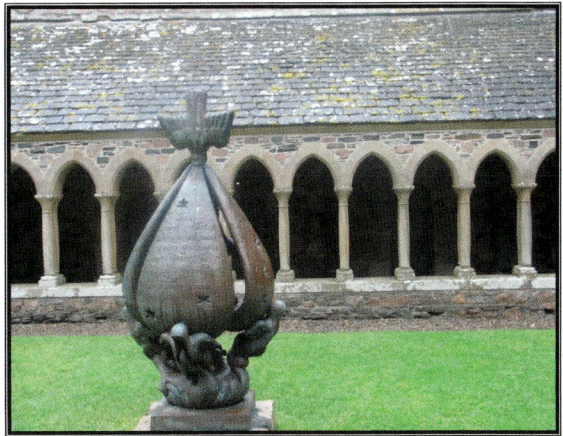

New Cosmology

"We either choose to come home to the cosmos to which we belong and to the planet that nurtures and sustains us, or our destiny on earth will continue to be one of alienation and self-destruction." [8]

With the development of evolutionary science and the new cosmology, Christian theology has had to resituate itself within a completely new world view. Most Christians have been willing to accept the Genesis story as myth not science, and to see God as the author of the evolutionary process. Most have long since ceased to believe in the biblical world view of a three-tiered Universe. Until recently, however, many theologians and preachers (including me) have been unwilling to grapple with the effect that this changing world view has on every aspect of Christian doctrine. We have been unwilling to hear the story of the Universe itself as it tells us how humans were shaped and fired in the same primordial furnace as stars, rocks, mountains, seas, plants, and animals.

Ecofeminist theology, on the other hand, endeavours to take seriously the need to blend science, religion, and poetry into a new understanding for our time. It calls us to outgrow our allegiance to the biblical world view of a six-day creation and a three-tiered Universe, and to construct a theology that arises from the Great Birth—"out of the point, the swelling, out of the swelling, the egg, out of the egg, the fire, out of the fire, the stars." [9] It calls us to leave behind a science that views Earth as barren mechanism and to embrace a sacramental perception which sees the Universe and all its processes as imbued with Spirit—God's transcendence utterly immanent in the materiality of all life.

Central to the new cosmology is the view that consciousness, understood as the inner intelligence that pushes life toward greater complexity and creativity, developed from *within* creation over fifteen billion years of evolution. Humans emerged from and with the Universe, are made of the same materials, and constantly interchange materials with other creatures. Ecofeminist theology takes this to mean, as the poet says, that

> Spirit is sleeping in the rock,
> dreams in the flower,
> awakens in the animal,
> and knows it is awake in the human. [10]

In ecofeminist theology, there are no opposing spheres, no dualism of spirit and matter. God is present in the Cosmos and the Cosmos is present in God. God is not apart from creation, but is the very process and energy that hold together the beauty and savagery of the universe.

Also central to the new cosmology is the relatedness of all creation in the web of life. This means that humans live our lives "in harmony with nature and its rhythms, with the cosmic process of order-disorder-interaction-new order that is taking place in each being," and that "the world and its creatures are within the human being in the form of the archetypes, symbols, and images that inhabit our interiority and with which we must integrate." [11] This paradigm of oneness in diversity and diversity in oneness shapes theology in new ways and creates a heart of wisdom.

It is this ecofeminist theology that I endeavour to bring to my life and ministry and which I describe in the following paragraphs.

God

> "...the whole universe, both matter and spirit is encompassed by the Matrix of the living God in an encircling that generates freedom, self-transcendence, and the future, all in the context of the interconnected whole." [12]

In order to speak about how I understand God out of my own experience and context, and in light of the new cosmology, I will tell a story. In the summer of 2007, my younger brother was waiting for a heart transplant, and early one morning I received word that a matching heart had been found and that Rob would be going into surgery later that day. It was the Monday of the July long weekend and I had just started my holidays at our cottage in

Haliburton County. Since traffic would be terrible on the holiday Monday, we decided to stay the night at the cottage and travel to London in the morning.

After making that decision, I went to sit by the river to pray. It was a beautiful, sky-blue and gold day, and the river was flowing with great energy. The birds were singing in the trees and the trees were sighing in the wind. I prayed by stilling and centring myself in the energy and beauty of creation and by opening myself to God's healing power in the Universe. In my imagination, I then wrapped my brother in that energy, along with the transplant team, my sister-in-law, niece and nephew, and the family in which a death meant that my brother would live.

At bed-time that night, I lit a candle in my room to remind me, whenever I woke, of the healing light and energy that were manifest in Jesus and which continue to be manifest in the world. I envisioned that light surrounding my brother while the surgery was taking place. During the night, I also continued to imagine the energy of the river, the strength of the pines, and the peace of the starry sky filling the Operating Room and everyone in it. When night-time worrying surged in, I kept opening myself to that energy and emptying myself of all fear. I was filled with a sense of confidence that all things would be well. And it was.

In the theology which has developed out of my life experience in conversation with cosmology, Jungian psychology, scripture, and the emerging Christian way, God is not a separate Being to whom I address my prayers. Rather, "God is "the power of life, energy, love, sustaining and energizing the web of life." [13] God is what we name the mystery of life—Being-itself, the life-force and energy of the Universe and everything in it. God is both transcendent and immanent in the bodies of all beings and in the body of Earth which make present the Divine as sacrament, as ethical concerns, and as communion. God is the energy that connects everything in the web of life, and "the primary and fundamental activity of the revealed God is relational." [14] Relationships—with the Divine, among people, in communities, and with Earth's other-than-human creatures—are central to waking a heart of wisdom and to the faith and spirituality of my elder years.

In this understanding, naming God is not about definition but about connection. All language for God is metaphorical— functioning as a means of relating us to all the ways that the divine energy may be known and accessed. In ritual and prayer, I image God in the fullest possible range of life forms—river, tree, light, Jesus, male, female, starry darkness—because that is where God is present, embodied, and known. I image God in the fullest possible range of relationships also—mother, father, brother, sister, guide, friend, love, saviour, justice—because that is where I experience the reality and diversity of our connectedness. And that reality is love in all its forms. So a rich diversity of God-language is foundational to getting a heart of wisdom and to my faith and spirituality as I age.

Jesus

> "...through Jesus [the entire universe] takes a leap forward and upward and offers the human mind a datum that it bore within itself but that had not yet emerged to exist." [15]

For me as a Christian, reflecting on Christology in light of the new cosmology, Jesus is the perfect embodiment of divine energy who becomes symbol and power for our own becoming. He is a "version of the structure of the universe: i.e.: simultaneously in the form of energy wave and material participle." [16] Like each of us, Jesus is a child of Earth and the Universe, belongs to the human family, and comes to his own self-awareness. In him, we see the completion of a new creation, the realization of God's reign, the unity of matter and spirit, and the fulfillment of inclusive community. His significance is not his maleness, but his humanity and his embodiment of the Divine which are a revelation of how each of us is also a unique embodiment of God.

His path illuminates the paths of other lives as a paradigm of inclusive relationships, of resistance to oppression, and of justice for all. He is central to my understanding of a heart of wisdom and of faith and spirituality in my elder years.

I understand Jesus, as Christ, to be filled with the energy that existed before creation—the energy that continues to create, uphold, and renew the face of the earth—the energy we name as God. Christ is the symbol of a new interiority and consciousness breaking forth in Jesus and continuing to be present to all humanity as the Universe expresses itself in a new way in human life. Christ is the energy that shaped the evolution of the Universe and which is internalized and lived by people of faith. He is central to my understanding of human beings and how we are called to be in transformational relationships.

From the point of view of the new cosmology, "the paschal mystery locates itself within the earth." [17] Jesus' death and resurrection flow from and are signs of the life-death-new life energy that has been present in the Universe from the beginning, and which is embodied in all things. His death and resurrection are not once and for all events for the salvation of the world, but a paradigm of the divine way of healing and salvation in the world.

The cross becomes a symbol of God's presence in the shattered and disgraced. It becomes a choice for Earth and its creatures, a sign of resistance to the powers of oppression, and a call to the life-style of self-giving needed to heal the Earth and bring justice to all its creatures. Resurrection is a metaphor for the energy of new life that is built into the fabric of creation. It is this energy for transforming individuals and society that I seek to live into and to help others live into so that we may awaken into a heart of wisdom.

The "lordship" of Jesus, I believe, does not arise from being unlike other humans as the only son of God, but from being *fully* human. It is an authority that arises from within—the authority of one who has fully realized his deepest self and has completely actualized the power of love. It is an authority that arises from being wholly for and with others in the web of life, and yet being subject to no other authority except the Divine within oneself.

As such, the "lordship" of Jesus is a paradigm for us to follow in saying no to patriarchal domination in every form, and in living our own true humanity as male and female, each with an unrestricted share in the mystery of life, in the experience of divine power, and in the doing of God's work. In my spiritual practice, I seek to know this Christ-power in my own life and to live it abundantly in community.

Trinity

> "Trinity is the expression of the Mystery, both one and multiple that envelopes us, that has made us what we are, and in which we participate ceaselessly." [18]

Trinity is a metaphor about the nature of God which derives from and points to a reality in the Universe, in Earth, in peoples and cultures, in human relationships and within every person. It is the reality of diversity in unity. It is the experience of the richness and complexity of all things within a unified whole.

In this understanding, Trinity is not the Being of Father, Son, and Holy Spirit, but rather a mode of divine being, a mode of our being, a mode of being of all creation—a reality that lives in us and we in it. Trinity points to our common origin, our shared substance, and our shared life in the immense diversity of all life. It is a way of understanding that to live is to be in relationships with others—to support and nurture life in community.

Humanity

> "...we are all one and the same Sacred Body in
> multiple and diverse expressions." [19]

From the perspective of my experience and context, including the new cosmology, I believe that to be human is to be "bodily-enspirited organisms...with particular responsibilities towards the sustaining of this life." [20] Like all other beings, we are creatures in the web of life and bear divinity in our bodies. Unlike other-than-human creatures, however, our experience of the beauty and brokenness, the communion and separation, the violence and wonder, the suffering and blessing of life leads us to conscious reflection on what it means to be human. It is this reflection that awakens into a heart of wisdom. Such reflection is central to my spirituality and faith as I age.

To be human is to live in awe and wonder at all the ways of divine embodiment in the world. To be human is to praise and give thanks for the bounty and benevolence of Earth in sustaining its creatures. To be human is to be accountable and proactive in our own becoming—to actualize, as fully as we are able, the divine life within us; and to support others and rejoice with them in *their* becoming. To be human is to be both enmeshed in and resistant to the powers of oppression and injustice, and to seek justice for Earth and all its creatures. To be human is to be in relation and to support and nurture life in community. One purpose of my spiritual practice is to deepen into my humanity. The ministry in which I am engaged is to enable people to develop their humanity in conscious wisdom.

**Iona
Pilgrimage**

Some Exercises for Exploring our Spirituality and Faith

1. Guided meditation: A Conversation with Jesus
   Come to the quiet in any way that is helpful for you.
   Imagine yourself walking on a beach...
   Hear the sound of the waves...
   Feel the sand under your bare feet...
   Feel the wind on your skin and the warmth of the sun...
   As you walk, you see a figure in the distance coming toward you...
   As you get closer, you realize that the person is Jesus.
   You greet him and the two of you sit together on a large flat rock...
   He looks at you with great love...
   He asks you, "Who do you say I am?"
   You respond...
   You have a conversation with him...
   When the conversation comes to an end, you say goodbye, and walk back down the beach...
   As you walk, you reflect on the conversation and what it means for your life...
   When you are ready, open your eyes...
   In your journal write the story of this encounter.

2. Spirited Conversations
   Sit with a trusted friend or convene a circle.
   Centre yourselves in the quiet.
   Pose a question such as:
   > What do you believe about the soul?
   > What do you believe about life after death?
   > Who is Jesus for you? The Trinity?
   > What are holy writings for you?
   > What is your image of God?
   > What is human life all about?

   One will speak from the heart out of one's own experience.
   The others will listen from the heart without interruption
   When the speaker is finished, sit in silence for a moment.
   The one who spoke will pose the same question to the one who listened or to the next one in the circle.
   When all have spoken, take time again in silence and then take 10 or 15 minutes to write in your journals.

3. A Cluster Exercise
   Cluster the words "life after death"
   Write a ten word synopsis based on your clustering.
   Express this insight in art.

4. Wisdom from Simeon
   Read the story of Simeon in Luke 2:25-35
   In your own words complete the sentence
   "Master, now you are dismissing your servant in peace,
   according to your word, for my eyes have seen...

5. A Psalm of Lament
   Write a psalm of lament to God about your life.
   > Invoke God's presence...
   > Cry out in lament
   > Ask for help...
   > Express your trust in God...
   > Make a vow...

6. Make a gratitude collage using images and words to express
   your thankfulness for your life and for the people who
   have been and are a part of it.

7. What is the place of
   the cross in your
   faith and spirituality?

   What is the place of
   the Church?

   How has or is this
   changing in your elder
   years?

   What do you need
   from the Church?
   What do you still want
   to give?

15. Meditation on Scripture

Choose a passage of text from the sacred writing of your tradition.

Quiet yourself with an entrance meditation of your design.

Use the process of *Lectio Divina* to engage the text.

Read the text aloud 3 times

First Reading: What words or images speak to me?

Second Reading: How is this passage speaking to my life today?

Third Reading: What am I being called to do?
                  How am I being called to change?

Respond to your reflection on the text.

Journal: 1. Free writing
                2. A dialogue with one of the characters in the story.
                3. Write a poem.

Movement: 1. Put on some drumming music and dance the story.
                2. Move as you imagine the characters in the passage might move.
                3. Act out the story.

Art: 1. Make a collage of images and words or phrases from the story.
                2. Use pastels to colour and give shapes to your feelings.
                3. Make an acrylic painting, simply allowing images and colours to pour through your hand.

                Use witness writing to respond to the images that you have created.

Notes:

Chapter Eleven
Going on as Fruit: *Gleaning and Passing on our Life's Wisdom*

Gleaning and passing on our life's wisdom is part of the work of conscious elderhood and this task is important not only for elders ourselves but for succeeding generations and for the life of the planet. Because we are living longer, we now have the opportunity to enjoy the fruits of our lives and leave them as a legacy for others, all in a way that those who preceded us did not. Gleaning our life's wisdom and passing it on "has a purpose that transcends personal motives. When we recount our life stories and mentor young people, we…refine all that we have done into its highest essence, so that our individual lives serve as blessings for future generations." [1]

When we tell our family stories, we pass on to the next generation the legacy of who we are, where we have come from, and what events have shaped us. We pass on the courage, faith, values, creativity, and passion that are in our bloodlines.

Gleaning my Life

A few years ago, I travelled to Britain and visited Biddulph Grange, the home of my grandmother on my father's side of the family. Mabel Heath was a woman from a wealthy upper class family. William Beattie was a middle

class Canadian clergyman who was studying on a scholarship at St. Andrew's College in Scotland.

Mabel and William both travelled to the Holy Land and met on a barge on the Nile River in Egypt. As improbable as the match seemed, they continued their courtship when they returned to

Britain and were married in 1905. After their marriage, my grandmother left her privileged life to come to Canada and live in the small town of Cobourg on the shores of Lake Ontario.

I had known this much of the story, but until I visited Biddulph Grange, I had never thought about the details of my grandmother's story. After seeing her birthplace, I tried to imagine what must have impelled her to abandon her privileged home. Did she feel stifled by the constraints of the life of a Victorian gentlewoman? Was she an adventurous woman longing for new vistas and a different life? Or was she simply a woman in love, willing to leave everything for the sake of a man?

Whatever the answer to these questions, Mabel Heath, her mother Laura, her sister Lolly, and her daughter Laura are women in my bloodlines. Their story is part of who I am, part of the legacy I can pass on to my nieces and now to my great niece.

Thinking about these women in my bloodlines, I wrote this poem.

Laura

My first name is Laura,
but to me Laura is
my crusty spinster aunt.
Dark-eyed and daunting,
she carried the name
in her generation,
synonymous
with the strength
of a woman alone,
and the haughty demeanour
necessary in a man's world.

The Laura before her
was Lolly,
also a spinster aunt.
A Victorian gentlewoman,
she practised the finer arts,
and painted country scenes
that glow with vitality and light.
I imagine her to be
like those paintings.

Before her
was another Laura
known to me only
as great-grandmother:
the wife of Robert Heath,
mother of Lolly, Mabel, Freddie,
Robert and Mary,
who died at age 47,
whose children arise up
and call her blessed,
whose husband also
praiseth her.

I carry the name
for my generation.
In bone and breath,
I carry Laura's strength,
Lolly's creativity,
Laura's blessedness.

The youngest Laura, my cousin's daughter,
is the present dark-eyed incarnation—
vivacious, intelligent, strong.

Such a heritage
I carry
and pass on,
in a name I do not use.

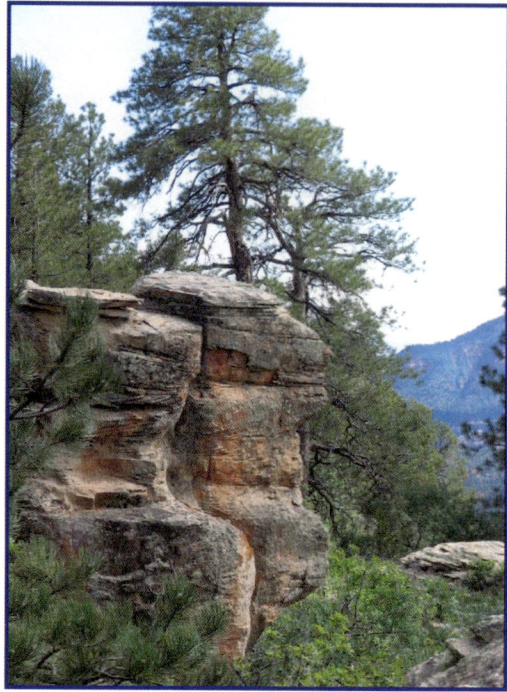

Elder Wisdom

During my Conscious Elderhood Vision Quest, I learned how other men and women were experiencing and living their elderhood. For the eleven days we were together in Colorado and Utah, I watched as the participants gleaned the wisdom of their life experience, discerned how they were being called to pass on this legacy, and ritualized, with courage and imagination, their intention to do so.

I listened to their stories as each one confronted elderhood in a unique way. Sitting in an ancient kiva, I participated with awe and gratitude in ceremonies which the questers had designed to mark their initiation into elderhood—ceremonies in which they danced, sang, prayed, drummed, and spoke the struggle and joy, the fear and hope of becoming and living as conscious elders.

I also watched as our guides modeled conscious elderhood and mentored the soul of our community so that each of the questers could do his or her inner work. I am deeply indebted to them for what I learned about the kind of wisdom that conscious elders glean from their life experience and how they pass it on to others.

When we become conscious, we find our own voices, for we have come to a place where we are no longer bound by the expectations of others or by social convention. We no longer care what others think, but are moved only by the dictates of our own souls. We no longer avoid speaking the truth for fear of hurting another or appearing foolish, but neither do we speak maliciously or without thought. When we become conscious, we use our voices in service of the community. We pass on our wisdom and speak up for justice and advocate for peace, and we no longer do it as we might have in years past, for affirmation or glory, but for the sake of generations to come.

Embodying fully our own faith and cultural traditions, we who become conscious elders speak our own truth, yet are open to the truth of others; we are passionate about what we believe, yet we have no stake in being right. We act upon our beliefs and hope to change the world, yet are detached from the outcomes of our action. Because our sense of self no longer depends upon getting the right result, we are content with what is, yet still strive for what might be. We are in love with the world as it is, but seek to make it a better place for our grandchildren and for generations yet to come.

When we become conscious in elderhood, we affirm the past and trust the future, but we live in the present. Grounded in the wonder and beauty of nature, we are open to gratitude and joy. Living in the moment, we are present to our own bodies and to our feelings, and have learned to breathe into discomfort or pain as an alternative to numbness. In our attentiveness to the moment, we are in deep communion with ourselves, with creation, and with God. We have learned to "be still, and know that I am God!"—to be still and know, to be still, to be. [2]

Having learned from the story of St. Martha, we befriend our dragons. Instead of trying to slay them as St. George did, we confront our dragons in the context of ritual and prayer, baptizing them as Martha did—in the name of the Holy. By engaging dragon energy with love through questions that lead to insight, those who become conscious are aware of our projections and have learned to withdraw them, turning the wounds of fire and talon into gifts of compassion and grace.

When we become conscious, we know how to die. Having confronted death over and over, we have learned to trust the cycle of birth, life, death, and rebirth. We know the truth of Jesus' words, "Unless a grain of wheat falls into the earth and dies, it remains just a single grain; but if it dies, it bears much fruit." [3] Having fallen into the darkness of accepting our own mortality, we have learned what death has to teach us—to live in the moment, to forgive and receive forgiveness, to make life-giving choices, to ask questions about life's meaning and purpose. Knowing that we will die, conscious elders have traded the generativity of work and body for the generativity of silence and soul that enables us to leave a legacy of a different kind.

Letting go of unfulfilled dreams and enjoying the true fruits of our labours, those of us who have done the work of conscious elderhood have come to terms with what we will leave behind in the world through our families and our work. We have had wonderful experiences for which we are grateful and we continue to seek the depths of our soul, but we know that we have been given these gifts for a reason and we stop seeking more and more experiences. We have learned that we are to use these experiences "to grow corn"—to create nourishment for ourselves and others. [4] Those of us who become conscious discover ways to use our wisdom for the sake of the community, for its youth, and for creation. We learn the task and art of mentoring both individuals *and* the soul of the community.

Mentoring the Soul of the Community

The guides on our Vision Quest modeled the mentoring of the soul of the community, and so I was able to discern some of its key characteristics. Chief of these is creating trust in such a way that individuals

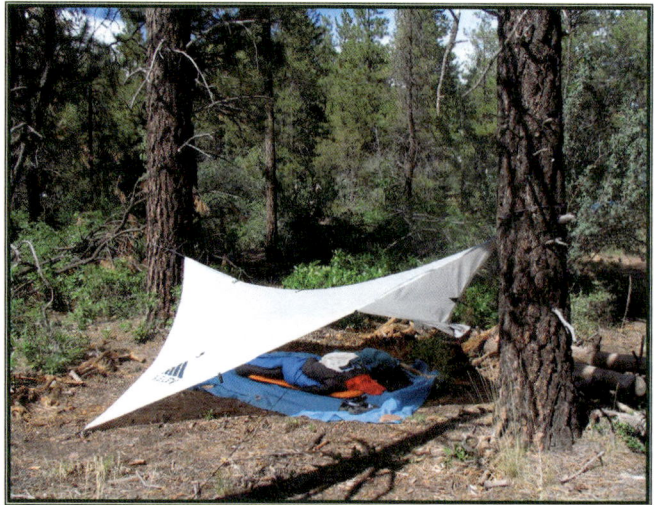

become a group, united in a common purpose and shared respect. Elders who have learned this skill are models of openness and vulnerability.

We share personal stories and wisdom when appropriate. We speak from the heart and listen from the heart, making ourselves wholly present. Passionate for the community and its work, elders who mentor the soul of the community hold themselves and others accountable to its purpose and rules, so that everyone can take part in the group in an atmosphere of safety and trust.

This ability to create trust is grounded in knowledge of group dynamics, but also in an experience of community which has given us the ability to sense the interactive field of the community. *"The Interactive Field is the dynamic interweaving of all the people in the [group], together with an ineffable presence that seems to guide [it] towards meaningful interaction."* [5](Author's italics) Those who become conscious develop an intuitive sense of the energy, the openness, the trust level, the unspoken tensions in a group and know when and how to intervene, when and why to hold back, and how to care for the soul of the community. Our consciousness has been deepened by our inner work so that we are able to embrace the group and individuals in it through this heightened awareness that enables listening with the ears of the heart.

Another gift of elders who mentor the soul of the community is a heightened awareness of the Sacred and an utter trust in its beneficent goodness. This trust enables us to create ceremony which connects the group to a greater reality. Those who become conscious in elderhood know how to make ceremonies in which it is possible to name fears and feelings, enact and embody purpose, weave a web of relationships, awaken gratitude, ground individuals in Earth's body and in their own bodies, foster cleansing and healing, and loosen the grip of cultural norms and expectations. In such ceremonies, the community is called to its mission and individuals have their gifts revealed by, valued for, and incorporated into that mission.

Elder mentors incorporate individuals into the community through story. The image of grandpa or grandma telling a story or of an elder at a campfire reciting the history of the tribe did not come about by accident or by Disney. Elders who mentor the soul of the community are storytellers, carrying in our memories a wide repertoire of life stories, sacred stories, and stories from various cultures. These stories enable individuals at various stages of life to find their story in the larger story of community and Cosmos, and also to recognize that larger story in their own stories.

Because we have lived through all the stages of life, and have done the work of each stage, those who become conscious in elderhood help others do the developmental work of soul at whatever stage they are at. Because we have lived long lives in a conscious relationship to the Divine, we know from within the various experiences of the spiritual journey and can help others along the way. Because we are invested in the community, we carry its sacred traditions and can help the community find its mission within the story which shapes its identity. Because we have become more open, we can also encourage the community to find new expressions of faithfulness in its particular time and place.

Conscious elders have learned to let go of ego's need for specific outcomes. Our identity is not tied up in whether the community succeeds in its mission, nor is our self-esteem dependent on whatever the community defines as success. Conscious elders can call the community to its soul calling precisely because we are not invested in what that calling is. With no fear of rejection or failure, we can be prophets or poets, caregivers or challenge-issuers as need decrees, mirroring back to the community its faithfulness or lack of it, trusting in God for the outcome, and relying on the soul and spirit practices of a lifetime to see us through to the end.

Mentoring the Young

We who become conscious elders glean our life's wisdom not only to mentor the soul of our community, but also to mentor the young. As we have quested for faith, meaning, and purpose during our own lives, so we invoke the spirit of the quest in the young. In doing so, we do not seek to inculcate our beliefs and values in those we mentor, but rather to call them into the heroic journey of finding their own way and living their own beliefs. We are midwives who labour with the young as they give birth to the fullness of their individual selves and offer their unique gifts for the sake of others.

Those who become conscious in elderhood may mentor the young in psychological and spiritual growth, in leadership development, faith formation, vocational training, and life skills. In each of these areas, we can pass on the wisdom we have gleaned from our life experience. "When an elder fertilizes a young person's aspiring mind with his knowledge and seasoned judgment, the student receives a living spark, a transmission that may one day blossom into wisdom." [6]

Using C.S. Lewis and the Irish tradition of the *anamchara* or soul friend, Edward Sellner develops the concept of spiritual mentoring. [7] From Lewis, Sellner learns that friendship is the *foundation* of mentoring, that the whole person is the *focus* of mentoring, that mentoring happens in many ways, that a mentor is *a fellow searcher*, that each person's way of mentoring is *unique*, and that mentoring is a form of *empowerment*.

From the concept of the *anamchara*, he learns that the attributes of a contemporary soul friend are maturity, compassion, respect for others, confidentiality, self-disclosure, theological reflection, and the ability to discern the movements of the heart. Sellner also offers some practical resources for discerning call and developing gifts for the ministry of spiritual kinship.

Mentoring, whatever form it takes, is always a two-way relationship.

> "The elder has more life experience and wisdom, so naturally the higher seeks it own level by flowing into the lower At the same time, the mentee, having more vitality, naturally rejuvenates and invigorates the elder with energy and an influx of fresh ideas. Without this exchange, the elder may remain locked in the past. With their penchant for experimentation and their forward-looking mentality, young people give elders the gift of encountering the present and anticipating the future. What mentees receive...is a readiness to bridge the past and the future." [8]

Gathering and passing on the fruits of our wisdom assures us that the meaning of our lives is joined with the eternal stream of history in the legacy which we send forward in the lives of the young in our family and community. We also contribute to the growing consciousness and wisdom of humanity and to the restoration of relationships and of the Earth.

Some Exercises for Gleaning and Passing on Your Life's Wisdom

1. The Speech of Your Life
   You have been asked to speak before the United Nations General Assembly. As you prepare your speech, you get in touch with your deepest convictions, the wisdom you have gained over your lifetime, and your hopes and dreams for the Earth.
   Visualize yourself proclaiming your vision to the leaders of the world.
   What do you say to them?
   How do you challenge them to take responsibility for the future of the planet?
   or
   You have been asked to speak at the Annual Meeting of your congregation. As you prepare your speech, you get in touch with your congregation's vision for its ministry in the community.
   You think about where it is being faithful and how you see it is falling short. You think of your hopes and dreams for them.
   Visualize yourself speaking. What do you say to them?
   How can you pass on this wisdom?

2. Passionate Issues List
   List 10 issues about which you are passionate and which will affect future generations.
   Choose one or two.
   Reflect on how you are making a difference.
   How are you bringing your elder-wisdom to this issue?
   How are you being called to serve the world, your community, your church, and your family through this issue? What actions are you being called to take?

3. Collage: Who I Am and What I Leave Behind
   Draw, paint or make a collage with symbols, words, and images that tell who you are, what you stand for, what legacy you leave behind.

4. Write Your Epitaph or Eulogy
   Write an epitaph or eulogy that tells the essence of what your life was about.

5. Letters to my Grandchildren (or the Young of the World)
   Write letters to your children and/or grandchildren passing on to them the wisdom you have learned over your lifetime.
   Tell them the prayers and dreams you have for them.

6. A Letter Writing Campaign
   Write letters to the editor or to members of government or corporate presidents about issues that concern you.

7. Family History
   Make a scrapbook or DVD of your family history and pass it on to your children.

8. Lectio Divina: Revelation 21:1-6 or Isaiah 58:6-9

First Reading:	Read the passage aloud. What word or phrase grasps me? Journal and/or draw.
Second Reading:	Read the passage aloud a second time. How is God speaking through this passage to my life today? Journal and/or draw.
Third Reading:	Read the passage aloud a third time. How is God calling me to change? What is God calling me to do? Journal and/or draw.

   Create a painting or collage based on your insights.

9. Conversation with Sacred Other
   Go to a place where the land or water bears the scars of humanity's abuse.

Quiet yourself in that place.

Look slowly around you, simply letting your gaze fall on whatever is before you. When something grasps your attention, engage it with all your senses.

Have a conversation with it. Tell it what's in your heart—what you are feeling and thinking.

Ask it what wisdom it would speak to you.

How is it calling you to action?

Write this dialogue in your journal.

10. The Way of Circle

Learn the ways of "circle" and teach it to others so that they can use it in leadership roles in your congregation or other organizations of which you are a part.

11. Moments of Faith

In your faith community, begin a program in which elders share the stories of their journey of faith in printed and/or spoken form.

12. Grandparents Helping Grandparents

Take part in an organization which helps grandparents in countries in the two-thirds world.

Form a chapter in your community.

13. Wisdom Circle

Gather a group of elders who will meet in a circle format.

Convene your circle with ritual.

Begin each gathering with a time of check-in when each member has an opportunity to tell about what is going on in his or her life.

Share leadership.

Use poetry, art, and stories to deepen into your elderhood.

End with a circle blessing.

14. Mentoring

Find an opportunity to mentor a young person—whether in your career field, in a faith community, in a school or in a volunteer organization.

15. Respond to the following image.

From Seed to Flower to Fruit

What did you receive as seeds in your life?
From whom did you receive them? Give thanks for those people.
What are you passing on as flower? As fruit?
To whom are you passing it on?

Notes:

Conclusion

The Journey Continues

This chapter is not, of course, the conclusion. In many ways, it is the beginning. The longing to become wise continues. The desire to be present to my life continues. The yearning to live, not out of my fear of failure, but out of my power continues. The commitment to creating a safe place for me and others to die continues. The journey toward conscious elderhood continues. What this final chapter will attempt to do, then, is not to make a definitive statement about conscious elderhood, but rather to reflect upon where I began the journey, what happened along the way, where I am now, and how I am envisioning the way forward.

This journey began with the recognition that my sadness at seeing the elderly, the experience of accompanying Mom on her final journey, and the beings of nature were calling me to confront my own aging. Along the way, an elderhood Vision Quest called me to live in the moment with attentiveness and compassion. A dead doe in the pampas grass taught me about creating a safe place to die. A milk bottle and a water bottle revealed a way of bringing together soul and spirit, and Christian spirituality and nature-based practices. A thickening body, painful joints, and a leaky bladder became the physical reality of growing older, and doctoral studies grounded me in the themes of conscious elderhood and their manifestation in my own life.

A Heart of Wisdom

My involvement in the Yearlong Soulcraft Immersion program of the Animas Valley Institute has been a significant part of my growth into a heart of wisdom. Not only did this group of women and one man bear witness to their own wise hearts, but they also mirrored to me what I had hoped, but did not really believe—that I am showing signs of wisdom.

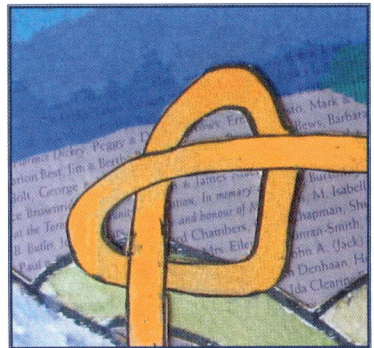

During the last gathering of our group which took place on a mesa in the Escalante region of Utah, our guides invited us to sit in pairs and mirror to one another our gifts and a challenge for the way ahead. If you have never done anything like this, I can tell you how difficult it is, but also how life-giving. For those of us who have trouble believing in and trusting our own beauty, it is a great gift to have it mirrored to us by others—especially when, as happened in this group—we each heard the same comments over and over.

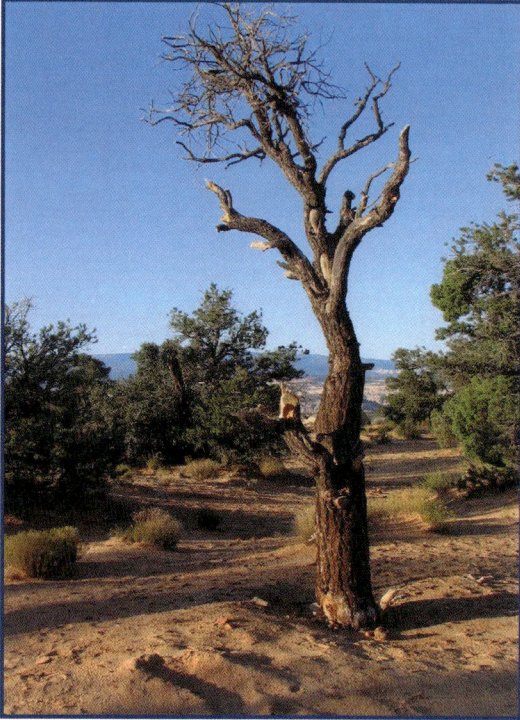

What I heard from each woman as we sat on the desert sand in the shade of ancient pines and junipers was an affirmation that this journey is teaching me to live in such a way that I am becoming wise. According to them, my presence is one of grace and gentle power. I radiate beauty, faith and peace. I live the Jesus-life and embody the Christian faith beautifully. I also embody elder wisdom and a child-like sense of playfulness.

Knowing myself from the inside out, I have trouble believing it when people say such things about me. I feel awkward writing them down, and I do so, not to suggest that I have arrived at a heart of wisdom, but only to bear witness to the fact doing this inner work really is transformative. I have changed and I will continue to change, not because it is me making it happen, but because it is the Divine Mystery who is the power in this transformation.

So I trust that the process of getting a wise heart will continue as I move into the really messy part of growing old—illness, loss, declining strength, loss of independence. I trust that what I have learned so far, the soul and spirit practices I have developed, and the unfolding that has already happened will enable me to keep on the path of consciousness in elderhood that leads to a wise heart.

A Safe Place to Die

In the mirroring of my gifts that took place in Escalante, one of the women said that I *am* a safe place to die, that my willingness to be vulnerable and my courage to dive in and bring stuff up to the light create safety for others to do the same. It was humbling to hear this, and at the same time daunting, for the challenge that lies ahead is to bring this gift back to the people among whom I serve. The challenge is to understand more fully what it will mean for these people to have a safe place to die and to find ways to make it happen.

I envision groups in which we study ecofeminist or "emerging church" theology and participants are threatened by new ideas. In such a group, creating a safe place to die will mean holding the space for confusion, fear, and even anger. It will mean challenging people to stay with these feelings and to endure the chaos. It will mean offering calm and understanding support in the midst of struggle. And it will mean rejoicing with them when they win through to a new understanding or accepting that the time is not ripe for transformation or that they just do not want to change.

I envision convening a Wisdom Circle in which those of "a certain age" covenant together to do the work of conscious elderhood. In this group, circle practice, storytelling, soul poetry, art, and ritual will be the means of creating a safe place for us to die into our elderhood. The elders of this circle will also seek to continue to grow, to mentor the young and the soul of our community, and to pass on our legacy through active involvement in issues about which we are passionate.

I envision pastoral care which creates a safe place for individuals to die from one stage of life to another by doing the inner work necessary for development. With children this will involve getting out into creation and activating their imaginations as well as their sense of awe and wonder. It will mean finding ways to help families teach their children the values, the stories, the customs, and the skills of living in family, in the culture, and in the faith community. With teens, it will mean making confirmation into a true passage into adulthood and finding other means of helping them to develop the skills which enable that passage. With adults, it will mean helping them to find their soul gifts and a way of delivering those gifts to the community. It will mean developing opportunities for mentoring and ways of being involved in transforming society. Finally, it will involve helping people at the end of life to die with courage, faith, and dignity.

Metaphors of Aging in Nature

When I began this work, I was seeing images of death and dying everywhere in nature, and it was these images which impelled me toward the work of becoming conscious in elderhood. Now, having done some of the work of coming to terms with my mortality, I see other images in nature. I see life coming out of death. I see endurance in the midst of storms and adaptability in the face of change. I see images of winter—of paring down and simplifying, of clarity and far-seeing, and of water running even in the midst of frost and ice.

I see weathered beauty in rock and wood. I see strength in weakness and breaking down in order to break open.

What I now discover in nature is my oneness with all creation—in life *and* in death. I feel a sense of communion with all the beings of earth and in this communion, a growing acceptance of my death simply as part of life.

In this communion, I am also discovering an ethic of awe and care for creation. I am filled with wonder at the intricacy and complexity of relationships in nature and at my place in those relationships. I am filled with anger and grief at what we humans, me included, are doing to creation, but I am not paralyzed. Confronting death has freed energy for life—mine and the whole Earth's.

Facing Debility and Death

While I am no longer obsessed by death, I do think about dying. I wonder what it will be like to become ill and how death will come to me. Both cancer and heart disease run in my family, and I imagine that one day I will be touched by one or the other, but I am no longer filled with dread. Instead, along with a niggling of fear, I feel curiosity and a sense of anticipation. I experience a marshalling of strength and a burgeoning of trust. Whatever comes, I will meet it with courage, faith, and the capacity to endure.

Facing death has freed energy for life. I am discovering a new capacity to be in the moment. I pay attention to my body and to the voices of other-than-human beings. I have less tolerance for what is trivial and trite, but a greater capacity to act upon my passions. I am less disturbed by differences, and more grateful for diversity and multiplicity. Facing death has led to an awakening of gratitude, of compassion, of purposeful living, and consciousness.

The journey ahead is one of deepening into this consciousness and integrating it more fully into my living. In the end, the proof of the pudding, as my father used to say, will be in the eating. But I believe that how I live now is how I will face my death, and I am content that all will be well.

Doing Everything with Soul

At the end of our Yearlong Soulcraft Immersion program, our guides gave us fifteen questions to write about spontaneously and share with one another by e-mail. All of the questions were about living with soul. One of the questions was: "What is the holy place that I occupy in the community of all life?

Doing everything with soul is about living from this place— the place that I and no one else can fill. This is what I wrote:

The holy place I occupy in the community of all life is called Anne
which means "the grace of God is with you."
It is a place of *presence*—
a unique manifestation of the Sacred in a woman
with a big body, a big heart, and a longing for wisdom.
It is a place of beauty *and* brokenness, of faith *and* fear.
I live in this place as an invitation –

to the granite strength of northern rock,
to the shaping power of the west wind,
to the immense clarity of sky,
and to the renewing life of water—
an invitation to all the amazing adventures of soul and spirit.
This grace-filled presence of me is my place;
it is what I offer to my people
and to the community of life.

Living into this place and presence of me is the challenge ahead in conscious elderhood. It will require being aware of those times when my fear of failure and of rejection are barriers to being fully present, to speaking my truth, to raising difficult issues, and to confronting death in me and in others. It will mean letting go of ego, control, and smallness and opening to soul, wildness, and largeness. It will mean bringing all of this to my work, my relationships, and to all the roles I play in each. It will mean being conscious in elderhood.

Coming to Terms with My Life

Coming to terms with my life is an on-going journey of healing. It is Loyal Soldier work. [1] It is the search for the Inner Beloved and the marriage of masculine and feminine within. It is searching through memory for the roots of brokenness and the genesis of beauty. It is deepening my awareness of when I am projecting my "stuff" onto other people and the work of withdrawing those projections. It is carrying my sacred wound with gratitude so that it becomes a source of blessing.

Practices that have been and will continue to be essential to this process are writing poetry, taking my inner work out onto the land, and seeing everything through the lens of life, death, and resurrection—both in creation and in Jesus Christ.

During our gathering in Anza Borrego State Park in California, I was doing work with my wounding around the body and realized that I carry not only my own wounds, but also those of my mother and grandmothers. I decided to walk with my grandmothers on the land, and found my way into a hidden canyon that snaked back up into the mountains. I walked with my grandmothers up the wash and felt their presence like two ancient native women whose relationship to this land was a source of healing and wholeness. The place I walked was a place of rock, sand and palm trees. I called it "Two Grandmothers Canyon."

As I walked, I reflected on the lives of my grandmothers, both of them born to privilege. One of them, however, after her marriage to my grandfather lived a hand-to-mouth existence. This was my mother's mother, and as I reflected on her life, I felt a connection to issues around sexuality and the body which my mother carried and which I carry also. I came to a knowing that my grandmother had also carried these same wounds, and out of that knowing, I wrote this poem which is helping me to come to terms with my body.

What I Heard in Two Grandmothers Canyon

Ancient lineage and proud family lines—
that was my heritage.
A pampered girl,
knowing nothing, I married for love.
Later, I became so angry at him.
That land was nothing
but blood and sweat and hard times,
and even that he farmed away.
Six children, every one of us working
and it still wasn't enough.
Bitter? You bet I was.
As prickly as that cactus
and growing in the same barren soil.

What did I know of a man's needs?
I was horrified and ashamed,
and finally glad that it was over.
Then came the surprise!
I was so angry.
He had to satisfy himself.
No matter what I thought or felt.
Another mouth to feed,
and Edna so out of joint

at no longer
being youngest.
But I taught them all to work.
They knew how to work, I'll say that.
What those boys were doing with their sisters
makes me sick.
If I'd known...Men!
What a sorry lot.
Then the sheep farm—stupid, smelly creatures!
Then house to house in the city,
one step ahead of the bill collector.

But I could have been less bitter,
made it easier,
learned to let go,
let myself be touched.
No! I was too stubborn,
too high miss-mighty.
And in the end I was untouched—
untouched and bitter,
now there's a combination.

Feeling my way, through poetry, into the wounding of the women in my bloodlines led me to another memory about my grandmother, and to another poem.

Behind the Door

I stand behind the door
watching,
a ten year old,
afraid to see,
yet drawn
by mystery and death.

My grandmother is dying.
In the den,
she's been dying for months.
In a hospital bed,
she's been nursed
by my mother,

the one she wanted
to be with her.
I hear the ratchet
of the stretcher unfolding,
the muted voices,
and Grandma's soft groan.

I am paralysed
invisible, voiceless,
wanting my mother,
wanting arms around me,
wanting words to comfort me
the living one.

But she is holding her mother,
speaking comfort
to the dying.

I remember neither
what came before,
nor what followed
this moment.

I remember only
this lost child,
alone
with feelings and fears
too big to comprehend,
too deep to be expressed,
too frightening to admit.

I feel her still inside me
her ache an abscess,
her heart a lonely hunger.

Since that day,
I have been hungering
for the beginning and ending
of this sorrow.
the beginning of awareness
and the ending of innocence,
the death of illusion
and the genesis of faith

Through the crack in the door
I see the child I was
and the woman I have become.
I feel arms enfold the girl,
hear soft answers
to anguished questions—
a mothering embrace
and wise womanly words.
My arms, my voice, myself
mothering
me.

This conversation with my grandmothers in the canyon and what I wrote afterward have resulted in a deep inner healing for me. I have experienced in my body the cycle of life, death, and new life, and I realize that my grandmothers and my mother experienced the living and the dying, but I am the one who has been graced to carry these forward into new life. I am the one who is being healed into my body, and I envision that in elderhood I will continue doing this work of coming to terms with my life, so that I and even my ancestors might be healed.

Discovering What I Yet May Be

Engaging in this work, both the work of conscious elderhood and the work of writing this book, has employed every aspect of my soul and spirit. I have moved within and discovered the beauty of who I am in a deeper way than ever before. With new confidence and purpose, I am finding ways to offer who I am— the wise woman I am and am becoming—as a gift to my community. I have sojourned in the wilderness as former spiritual practices and understandings crumbled and I have won through to a faith that sustains me and in which I experience a new sense of oneness with the Divine Mystery in all things. And if all this is any indication of what lies ahead, I know that there is much more yet to come. I am filled with excitement, gratitude, and a sense of adventure.

I have no idea for certain what lies ahead, but I do know that the pathway lies through exploring my creativity more deeply through photography, painting, and writing. The pathway lies through engaging Christ consciousness more fully through bringing nature-based practice more intentionally into my ministry, and through practical involvement in environmental issues. With all this ahead, who knows what I yet may become?

Spirituality and Faith

One of the lessons I have learned on my journey is to be at peace with not knowing, while at the same time seeking to embody fully what I believe to be true. I feel comfortable with my understanding of God, while acknowledging that the Divine Mystery is so much more than my little imagining.

I see myself as one of many looking through knotholes in a fence at what is happening on a baseball diamond. I see what is happening in centre field, at second base, on the pitching mound, and at home plate, but I am mistaken if I imagine that this is all there is to the game. When I tell what I see to others and they tell what they see to me, we have a more complete picture.

So I will continue to deepen into my own knowing, realizing that it is partial and provisional. I will listen to the wisdom and experience of others and create opportunities to share my ecofeminist spirituality with them in the hopes that all of us will open more fully to the Mystery whom we call God in the Christian tradition.

During our Yearlong Soulcraft Immersion program, I was in constant awe of the gratitude which many of the participants brought to ritual and to the living of their lives. Thankfulness overflowed for the freely-given beauty and bounty of the Earth in its Antelope Island, Anza Borrego, Abajo, Escalante, and Temagami manifestations. Gratitude for love in all its manifestations, for the blessedness of being alive, and even for one's sacred wounding was a constant stream flowing through all our ritual and in our circle sharing.

In elderhood, I want to deepen into this practice of gratitude, so that whatever lies ahead I will meet it with a sense of the abundance of grace, not its scarcity. As one who is prone to see the glass as half-empty, rather than half-full, this will be a challenge, but I am determined to sing my way home with joy and gratitude.

I am also determined to deepen into the practice of self-designed ritual. As I wrote this book, I had the worship centre pictured here on my desk. In it are pieces of my story, bits of my longing, rocks from my sacred places, and talismans of my faith and of my relationships with others. Each object reminded me of the giftedness of my life experience and I felt the power of these connections flowing through me as I wrote.

It is this connectedness to the Divine through ritualizing our experience that I will bring to the people among whom I minister. I want each of them to know what I know—that the Divine is present and flows in each of us as a river of goodness and power, offering to us, in every moment, the peril and promise of fully inhabiting our lives.

Gleaning and Passing on My Wisdom

For me, *gleaning* my life's wisdom is not the issue. Passing it on is another matter. As an introvert intuitive, I have always been better at dreaming possibilities than enacting practicalities. My call in elderhood, then, is to move more deeply into the practice of passing on my life's wisdom.

In one sense, this is what my vocation as a minister is all about—distilling the essence of the Christian tradition and teachings, as well as my own and others' experience, and offering it as life-giving water through preaching, liturgy, teaching, and pastoral care. As I grow into my elderhood, however, I want to be more conscious of my role as a mentor of individuals and of the soul of the community. I want to create opportunities, not only for me but for others, to engage in life-giving relationships in which we accompany the young into the fullness of their lives.

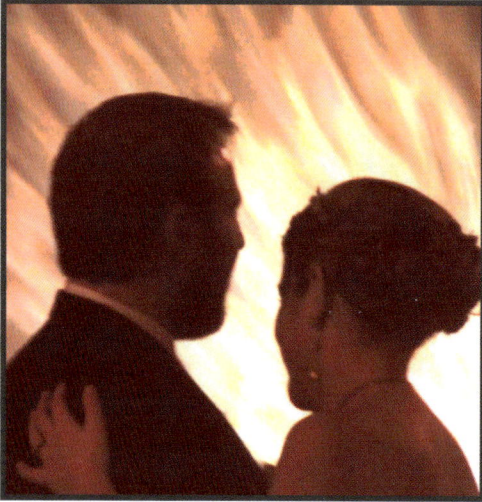

With the marriage of my nephew and the birth of my great-niece in 2007, I became aware of new opportunities to share our family stories and also my own wisdom.

At Ben and Kelly's wedding, I was able to blend their spirituality, values and understanding of marriage with my own wisdom, faith, and life experience. Bringing all of this together with imagery of landscapes sacred to each of them, I created a marriage service that spoke about the beauty of life, the joys and struggles of relationships, and the mystery of the Divine.

When my great-niece was born, her mother asked if I would baptize Mya, but because she and her partner are not Church members and do not practice the Christian faith, I said no. Later, I realized that just because I would not baptize Mya, it didn't mean that we could not do something. So I organized a baby blessing ritual to which we were each asked to bring something for the baby—something that would connect her to the Beattie and the Wolfe family stories, something that would tell her where she came from and help her discover who she is—something that will bless her and accompany her on her life journey.

There are more weddings planned in my family and there will be more babies born, and I look forward to discovering more ways of gleaning and passing on our family stories and my own life-wisdom in that context.

I also envision a continuing and deepened ministry of mentoring in my congregation. My experience to date has been that in every congregation I have served, there has been a least one person with whom I had a mentoring relationship of deep significance for both of us. These usually happened by chance rather than by design, but the way ahead now calls me to a greater intentionality both in mentoring individuals and in mentoring the soul of the community.

I dream of a Mentoring Program in which elders are trained to mentor others into faith and into leadership roles in the church. I envision a Wisdom Circle of elders who will meet together to discern how to hold the community accountable to its vision and to unite people in common mission and shared respect. I dream of a Story Project in which younger members of the congregation listen to and record the stories of elders as a way of helping them to discern and pass on their life's wisdom.

I dream…and dreaming I am connected to the circle of life that runs through me and through all the Earth.

And the journey continues.

The Journey Goes On

How are you envisioning the journey ahead into elderhood?
What do you hope lies over the horizon?

May you discover your heart's longing and the fullness of your life in conscious elderhood.

Notes:

Appendix A: Elder Tales

The Builder Has a Dream

$\bigcirc$nce upon a time, long ago and far away, there was an old man who had lived his life as a builder, carefully crafting homes for people out of wood which he hewed from the forest and stone which he quarried from the mountains. He and his wife lived contented lives, for he not only built sturdy homes on solid foundations, but he also had the happy trait of building strong relationships. As long as he was busy transforming wood and stone from the Creator's good earth into places of shelter and warmth, he lived contented. But as happens to those who are fortunate, the builder grew old and the day came when his gnarled hands could hardly saw a board or drive a nail. But he kept working, because that was what he knew. Being a builder was his life.

Then one night, the builder had a dream. He was walking down a street in the town where he grew up, passed houses he had built, when he met an old man wearing a sombrero. The man's face was wrinkled like an apple doll, but his eyes were clear and his gaze deep. He looked into the builder's face and said, "We have to talk."

Saying nothing more, the old man led the builder through a maze of back streets to the very edge of town. There, on a little lane which the builder had never known existed, was a house like none he had every seen—certainly like none he had ever built.

Light shone from every window and all the windows were round like bright eyes looking on the world with immense wonder. Gingerbread trim decorated every eave and rainbow colours painted every board. It was a child's playhouse grown to full size.

Music poured out the open door, and inside the house the builder could see children dancing. A little boy ran from the house and threw his arms around the builder, "I've been waiting for you. Come and dance."

"But I don't know how," said the builder.

"Yes, you do," said the boy, "you've just forgotten," and he pulled the builder into the house where they danced so beautifully that everyone stopped to watch and clapped their hands in joy.

As the music swirled to an end, the builder leaped high, clicked his heels together in sheer exhilaration, and with a start jolted awake in his own bed.

The next morning, the builder went back to his everyday life, but the old man in the sombrero and the little boy who danced were always with him. So he worked less and danced much, and whenever he danced, he felt contented. And that was often.

The Woodcutter Sees His Future

Once upon a time, an old man lived with his wife at the edge of an enchanted forest. All his life long, the man had cut firewood from the forest and sold it to the people of the village. He had learned from his father who had learned from his father that wood from this forest had magic properties when cut with a loving heart.

So the woodcutter had learned to sharpen his axe with a song of joy in his heart. He had learned to thank the spirit of the tree for offering its life, and he had learned to split the wood with a prayer for whatever family would burn it.

Consequently, wherever people knelt reverently to light a fire with that wood, houses would stay warm through the night, bread from the oven would taste like heaven, and those who sat near the fire would feel their hearts strangely warmed.

Over the years the woodcutter had come to know the forest like his own front room. He knew where the big oaks and maples had fallen and where the dead birches awaited the axe. What he harvested, he replaced, and his own sons and daughters he taught the ways of the forest and the skills of the woodcutter.

One day he entered the woods and followed his usual path through the trees, intending to cut up a big fallen oak he had seen the day before in a clearing in the heart of the woods. As he walked deeper and deeper into the woods, the air became dark and heavy and he could sense a storm approaching. The trees closed in around him, until the path he was following was merely a deer trail. Soon he was lost.

Nothing was familiar. There was no trail worn by generations of feet, no tall pine with a peculiar bole on its trunk, no giant beech with lovers' initials carved in it, only a thick, dark wood like none he had ever seen. The woodcutter was not so much frightened as perplexed. How could he lose his way in a place he had known all his life? Why had he never seen this part of the wood until now?

Eventually, scratched and tired, the woodcutter pushed his way into a small clearing ringed by tree trunks which crowded together as if leaning in for warmth. In the middle of the clearing, a fire was burning, the flames casting shadows that danced in the circle of trees. The place reeked of a magic stronger than any the woodcutter had ever experienced.

"What can this place be?" he wondered out loud.

As he spoke, a figure appeared in the flames and stepped from the fire. He was wizened and stooped, wrinkled of face and white of hair, clearly of man of great age, wisdom, and power. "This is the place where you meet your future," the ancient one said. "Come and see." And he stepped back into the fire and disappeared.

The woodcutter was beginning to be frightened, but his curiosity drew him to the fire and looking into the flames, he saw a hand beckoning him. Now the old woodcutter still loved an adventure and he said to himself, "This is deep magic. How can I turn away?" And he, too, stepped into the fire.

Immediately, the woodcutter found himself on a mountaintop overlooking a vast, strange land. The ancient one stood beside him. Turning to him, the woodcutter asked, "How can this be my future? I know nothing about such deserts and valleys!"

"Ah," said the ancient one, "but you know the magic of the forest, how to cut the wood that warms the soul."

"But what good will that do me?" asked the woodcutter. "There are no trees for miles in any direction."

"You will learn that as you travel," said the ancient one, "I have come to give you a token that will help you remember what you know. Give me your hand." The woodcutter stretched out his arm and the ancient one laid in his palm a tiny tree made of gold, hanging on a fine gold chain.

Suddenly there was a great flash of light. Then everything went dark and when the woodcutter could see again, he was lying in the shelter of an ancient oak tree.

"How strange," he thought. "I must have fallen asleep." But he looked down at his arms and saw that they were scratched and bleeding. He opened his hand and saw there a tiny gold tree hanging on a fine gold chain.

The old man returned to his wife and never again went into the forest to cut wood. Instead, he told stories about the magic of wood to anyone who wanted to listen. These stories warmed people's hearts and gave them hope. Whenever he spoke, the old man's hand was at his neck, turning over and over in his fingers the tiny gold tree that hung there. As he spoke, his eyes would dance like firelight.

Thus the woodcutter lived joyously to a ripe old age and died in peace.

The Woodcarver and the Child

Once upon a time, a poor woodcarver lived with his wife in a tiny house overlooking the water. The old man had spent his life making beautiful carvings, some of which he sold, but most of which he gave away. Hence, the carver and his wife were poor in goods, but rich in love.

Some of the people who bought the carvings displayed them in their homes and bragged about knowing the artist. Others carefully wrapped them in tissue paper and put them away for safekeeping. But those who received the carvings as gifts were moved by them in ways they often could not understand. Many of them touched their carvings so often in joy or sorrow, in gratitude or supplication that the wood began to glow with a patina beyond even the woodcarver's skills.

For years the woodcarver had been crafting a special project, a nativity set, and in his old age, it was nearing completion. The faces of Mary and Joseph were filled with such tenderness that only unloved or bitter hearts did not feel their eyes prick with tears. The shepherds' bodies were transfixed with such wonder that it was a hard heart indeed that did not sing. The wise men were so regal in their bearing that everyone instinctively stood straighter and returned home different people.

The woodcarver hoped to sell the set for enough money so that he and his wife could live comfortably in their old age and, as luck would have, a rich collector came into his workshop one day when he was working on the final piece—the tiny child in the manger.

So exquisite was the detail of this carving that the collector gasped and then slyly composed his face in an effort to hide how much he coveted the set. But the carver was not fooled and struck a hard bargain—enough to keep him and his wife comfortable as long as they lived. The two men agreed that the collector would pick up the nativity set in a week's time.

Every day during the next week the old man worked on the figure of the baby, but his heart was strangely heavy. Every day a little girl from the village came and watched him work, her eyes glowing as she saw the tiny, perfect form take shape. Every day, when the carver laid down his tools, she would gently trace her fingers over the head, the arms, the body that had taken shape that day. Man and child never spoke, but at that last moment of the day, each was filled with silent joy.

At last, on the day before the collector was to arrive, the baby Jesus was complete—a beautiful, laughing child with his arms outstretched and his hands open, as if to embrace all he could see.

"Oh!" sighed the girl, tears rolling down her face.

"What is it, little one?" asked the carver.

"He's the one," she replied, "I just know it."

"Whatever are you talking about?" queried the old man.

The little girl's tears flowed harder and her words came out on broken breaths. "It's my mother. They say she's dying, but I just know that if she could have the baby on the window ledge where she could see him, she would get better."

"Well, then, my love," said the carver, pausing only for a moment, "your mother shall have him," and he pressed the tiny figure into her hands.

The collector returned on the seventh day and, as you can imagine, flew into a rage when he was told that the nativity set was incomplete. The sale was lost and the carver felt sure that he and his wife would live in poverty until they died.

But word of his generosity spread throughout the village and the carver was honoured by all. He and his wife wanted for nothing and lived surrounded by love for the rest of their days.

The Old Woman and the Sea

Long ago and far away, an old woman lived by the sea. She had not always lived by the water, but had spent most of her life near the forest. There she had worked and married and raised her family. But her children had moved away, as children do, and her husband had died, as husbands do, and she became old, as all of us do. So she moved to a little house by the seashore to be near her children.

First thing every morning, the old woman sat in a solitary chair outside her front door and watched the sky over the sea. Though she was not accustomed to sitting and didn't know the ways of the sea, she learned this quietness in order to see what the clouds and wind and water might show her

If the day promised fair, she would go down to the shore and try her hand at fishing. Before long, she was able to cast her nets into the water and catch the fish that sustained her existence. Some of the fish was the daily food that kept her alive, for she knew that she had to eat every day. Some of the fish she salted away to keep her during the lean months, for in her childhood she had learned from her own mother to be frugal. But because she had also learned to be generous, she would take some of the fish into town to share with her friends and neighbours.

Though she made the best of it, the shore was not home; the water was not her chosen element and the old woman sometimes felt like a stranger in a strange land, an immigrant far from home, a person displaced from all she knew and loved. Still, she continued to fish and the sea fed her, and the little she had she shared with others.

One day, the old woman's net caught a fish such as she had never seen before. On its head was a jester's cap, complete with bells, and in its fins the fish juggled five round crystals. Much to the woman's astonishment, though by this time in her life, she had seen many things that could not be explained, the fish spoke.

"Dear lady, I bring you wisdom from the depths—and a gift. Take these crystals and hang them in the window of your house. Keep them shining brightly and they will bring you comfort and joy."

So the widow did as she had been told. By day the crystals reflected the light of the sun and made rainbows on the walls of her rooms. By night, they gathered up the light of stars and moon and brightened the darkness of her tiny home.

In the daytime, children came to visit to watch the rainbows arc across the walls and they brought her bits of ribbon and candy from their pockets. At night, fishermen out on the sea used the light of the crystal balls as a beacon to guide them safely to shore, and they shared their fish with the old woman.

So, even though she became too old to fish herself, she lived in comfort and peace until the day she died.

The Owl and the Ring

Once upon a time in a far away place, a man and his wife lived beside a clear stream that flowed out of the mountains. The windows of their home looked toward the mountains on one side and over the valley on the other. The door opened toward the water that sang its way over river stones.

Their house was filled with the changing colours of light as the sun first painted the tops of the mountains pink, then rolled down across the valley in waves of green and gold, and finally dipped behind the far hills, shading the land deep purple and blue.

It was in these hues that the man had found his livelihood, creating beautiful windows filled with all the colours of creation. Everyone who lived in a home or worshipped in a church with such a window felt a daily sense of encouragement and support, as though the window itself opened into the heart of God.

One day when the man had grown older, he hiked up the path along the stream to his favourite rock high up on the mountain side. The rock towered above a certain dark pool into which the water cascaded in a gossamer veil from high above. From his perch on the rock, the man watched either the falling water or the light over the valley. Here he found inspiration for his work.

This day as he contemplated the falling water, an owl flew from behind the shining shroud of water, perched in a nearby tree, and stared at him with unblinking eyes.

"It is time," the owl intoned, and flew back into the mist.

The man blinked to clear his eyes. "I must have fallen asleep and dreamed the owl," he thought." But nonetheless he walked to the tree and searched the ground underneath it. Right below the branch in which he had dreamed the owl were pellets—bits of bone and beak, fur and feathers such as an owl regurgitates after eating.

The man stirred the pellets and in the midst of them saw a glint of light. It was a gold ring, shining there among the leavings of the owl.

Overjoyed, the man hurried home to his wife and announced that he would never work again. In response to her questions he simply said, "It is time."

"But how will we live?" she asked.

Then he told her the story of the owl and showed her the gold ring.

"One gold ring won't keep us for very long," she scoffed.

"Maybe the ring is magic," replied her husband. "Put it on a make wish.

The woman put the ring on her finger and, feeling remarkably silly, wished for enough money to buy food for the week. In an instant, silver coins appeared on the table before them.

From that time forward, the man and woman never wanted for anything. They were remarkably generous to their friends and neighbours and became known for their open hands and hearts.

So they lived in comfort and peace, enjoying life, until they died at a ripe old age.

Notes:

Notes

Introduction
[1] www.animas.org

Chapter One: The Journey Begins
[2] Quoted in George E. Vaillant, *Aging Well* (New York: Little, Brown and Company, 2002), 249
[3] Psalm 90: 12, NRSV
[4] Ephesians 4:15, NRSV
[5] Dawna Markova, *I Will Not Die an Unlived Life* (York Beach, Maine: Conari Press, 2000), 1

Chapter Two: Metaphors of Aging in Scripture and Experience
[1] Psalm 19:1-4, NRSV

Chapter Four: Practices for Soul and Spirit
[1] Bill Plotkin, *Soulcraft: Crossing into the Mysteries of Nature and Psyche* (Novato, California: New World Library, 2003), 31
[2] Job 12:7-8, NRSV
[3] Psalm 19:1, NRSV
[4] Proverbs 6:6, NRSV
[5] John 1:14, NRSV
[6] Jack Zimmerman and Virginia Coyle, *The Way of Council* (Ojai, California: Bramble Books, 1996), 5-6
[7] Clara Pinkola Estes, *Women Who Run with the Wolves: Myths and Stories of the Wild Woman Archetype* (New York: Ballantyne Books, 1992), 462
[8] James Hollis, *Tracking the Gods: The Place of Myth in Modern Life* (Toronto: Inner City Books, 1995), 15
[9] Plotkin, 206
[10] Parker J. Palmer, *A Hidden Wholeness: The Journey Toward an Undivided Life* (San Francisco: Jossey-Bass, 2004), 90ff
[11] Estes, 299
[12] Plotkin, 207
[1] Patrice Malidoma Somé, *The Healing Wisdom of Africa: Finding Life Purpose Through Nature, Ritual and Community* (New York: Jeremy P. Tarcher/Putnam, 1999), 143

2 Stephen Gilligan, *The Courage to Love: Principles and Practices of Self-relations Psychotherapy* (New York: W.W. Norton & Company, 1997), 179

3 Hollis, *Tracking the Gods*, 17

4 Somé, 152

5 Robert Johnson, *Inner Work: Using Dreams and Imagination for Personal Growth* (New York: HarperSanFrancisco, 1986), 21

6 ibid., 10

7 Jill Mellick, *The Art of Dreaming: Tools for Creative Dream Work* (Berkeley: California: Conari Press, 2001), 180-182

8 James Hollis, *Mythologems: Incarnations of the Invisible World* Toronto: Inner City Books, 1995), 74

9 Psalm 46:4, NRSV

10 Micah 6:8, NRSV

11 Pat Allen, *Art is a Spiritual Path: Engaging the Sacred Through the Practice of Art and Writing* (Boston and London: Shambala, 2005), 61ff

Chapter Six: The Tree in Winter: *Facing Debility and Death*

12 Zalman Schachter-Shalomi. *From Age-ing to Sage-ing: A Profound New Vision of Growing Older* (New York: Warner Books, 1995)

13 ibid., 82.

14 Joanna Macy and Molly Young-Brown, *Coming Back to Life: Practices to Reconnect our Lives, Our World* (Gabriola Island, BC: New Society Publishers, 1998), 27

4 Mary Oliver, *New and Selected Poems: Volume One* (Boston: Beacon Press, 1992), 10

Chapter Seven: Like the Trees: *Doing Everything with Soul*

1 Palmer, 21

2 David G. Hallman, *Spiritual Values for Earth Community* (Geneva: WCC Publications, 2000), 60

Chapter Eight: Fallen Leaves: *Coming to Terms with our Lives*

1 Erikson, Erik H. and Joan Erikson, *The Life Cycle Completed.* (New York: W.W. Norton & Company, 1977), 126
2 Richard N. Wolman, *Thinking With Your Soul: Spiritual Intelligence and Why It Matters* (New York, New York: Harmony Books, 2001), 93
3 Anthony DeMello, *Sadhana A Way to God: Christian Exercises in Eastern Form* (New York: Image, 1984), 73
4 Roy Oswald, *Clergy Self-Care: Finding a Balance for Effective Ministry* (Bethesda: the Alban Institute, 1991), 159
5 ibid., 205
6 Terrence Real, *How Can I Get Through to You?: Closing the Intimacy Gap Between Men and Women* (New York: Fireside, 2002), 210

Chapter Nine: Still Green: *Discovering What We Yet May Be*

7 David Whyte, *The Heart Aroused: Poetry and the Preservation of the Soul in Corporate America* (New York: Doubleday, 1994), 109
8 Ephesians 4:13, NRSV
9 Real, 76
10 Allan B. Chinen, *In the Ever After: Fairy Tales and the Second Half of Life* (Wilmette, Illinois: Chirion Publications, 1994), 33-34
11 Holy Bible, NRSV

Chapter Ten: The Tree of Life: Spirituality and Faith

1 Schachter-Shalomi, 280
2 Sallie McFague, *Life Abundant: Rethinking Theology and Economy for a Planet in Peril* (Minneapolis: Fortress Press, 2001), 134-135
3 Diarmuid O'Murchu, *Evolutionary Faith: Rediscovering God in our Great Story* (Maryknoll, New York: Orbis Books, 2003), 70
4 Thomas Moore, *The Soul's Religion: Cultivating a Profoundly Spiritual Way of Life* (New York, N.Y.: Perennial, 2002), 129
5 Philippians 4:5, NRSV
6 Wayne Muller, *How Then, Shall We Live?: Four Simple Questions That Reveal the Beauty and Meaning of Our Lives* (New York:

Bantam Books, 1996), 221
[7] Jim Marion, *Putting on the Mind of Christ: The Inner Work of Christian Spirituality* (Charlottesville, VA: Hampton Roads Publishing, 2000), 58.
[8] O'Murchu, 30
[9] Starhawk, *Truth or Dare* (New York: Harper & Row, 1987), 1
[10] qtd in Leonardo Boff, *Cry of the Earth, Cry of the Poor* (Maryknoll, New York: Orbis Books, 1997), 69
[11] ibid., 216
[12] Elizabeth A. Johnson, *Women, Earth, and Creator Spirit* (New York: Paulist Press, 1993),43
[13] Mary Grey, *Sacred Longings: The Ecological Spirit and Global Culture* (Minneapolis: Fortress Press, 2004), 134
[14] ibid., 77
[15] Boff, 177
[16] ibid., 177
[17] James Conlon, *Earth Story Sacred Story* (Mystic, Connecticut: Twenty-Third Publications, 1994), 92
[18] Ivone Gebara, *Longing for Running Water: Ecofeminism and Liberation* (Minneapolis: Fortress Press, 1999), 153
[19] ibid., 82
[20] Grey, 133

Chapter Eleven: Going on as Fruit: *Gleaning and Passing on our Life's Wisdom*

[1] Schachter-Shalomi, 56-57
[2] Psalm 46:10, NRSV
[3] John 12:24, NRSV
[4] Story told by Ron Pevny on an Animas Valley Institute Conscious Elderhood Vision Quest, June 2005
[5] Zimmerman and Coyle, 99
[6] Schachter-Shalomi, 190-191
[7] Edward C. Sellner, *Mentoring: The Ministry of Spiritual Kinship* (Cambridge, Massachusetts: Cowley Publications, 2002)
[8] Schachter-Shalomi, 192-193

Conclusion

[1] Bill Plotkin, *Soulcraft: Crossing into the Mysteries of Nature and Psyche* (Novato, California: New World Library, 2003), 91-96

Bibliography

Art as a Spiritual Practice

Allen, Pat B. *Art is a Spiritual Path: Engaging the Sacred through the Practice of Art and Writing.* Boston: Shambala, 2005

Azara, Nancy. *Spirit Taking Form: Making a Spiritual Practice of Making Art.* York Beach, ME: Red Wheel, 2002

Coupar, Regina. *The Art of Soul: An Artist's Guide to Spirituality.* Ottawa, Ontario :Novalis, 2002

Degler, Teri. *The Fiery Muse: Creativity and the Spiritual Quest.* Toronto: Random House of Canada, 1996

Fox, Matthew. *Creativity: Where the Divine and the Human Meet.* New York: Jeremy P. Tarcher-Putnam, 2002

Huey-Heck, Lois and Jim Kalnin. *The Spirituality of Art.* Kelowna, BC: Northstone Publishing, 2006

Keely Wilson, Elizabeth. *Kaleidoscope: artistic techniques for the creative soul.* Danville, California: Brookside Press, 2000

Malchiodi, Cathy A. *The Soul's Palette: Drawing on Art's Transformative Powers for Health and Well-Being.* Boston: Shambala, 2002

McNiff, Shaun. *Art Heals: How Creativity Cures the Soul.* Boston: Shambala, 2004

Richardson, Jan L. *In Wisdom's Path: Discovering the Sacred in Every Season.* Cleveland, Ohio: The Pilgrim Press, 2000

Williams, Heather C. *drawing as a sacred activity: simple steps to explore your feelings and heal your consciousness.* Novato, California: New World Library, 2002

Circle Practice

Baldwin, Christina. *Calling the Circle: The First and Future Culture,* New York, New York: Bantam Books, 1998

Zimmerman, Jack and Virginia Coyle. *The Way of Council.* Ojai, California: Bramble Books, 1996

Conscious Elderhood

Arrien, Angeles. *The Second Half of Life: Opening the Eight Gates of Wisdom*. Boulder, Colorado: Sounds True, 2005

Chinen, Allan B. *In the Ever After: Fairy Tales and the Second Half of Life*. Wilmette, Illinois: Chirion Publications, 1989

_____. *Once Upon a Midlife: Classic Stories and Mythic Tales to Illuminate the Middle Years*. United States of America: Xlibris Corporation, 2003

Chittister, Joan. *The Gift of Years: Growing Old Gracefully*. Ottawa: Novalis, 2008

Dass, Ram. *Aging and Change: Omega Aging Conference*. Palm Springs, California: Ram Dass Tape Library, May 1, 1992

_____. *Changeless Aging*. Palm Springs, California: Ram Dass Tape Library, 1995

Erikson, Erik H. and Joan Erikson. *The Life Cycle Completed*. New York: W.W. Norton & Company, 1977

Feinstein, David and Peg Mayo. *Rituals for Living and Dying*. New York: HarperCollins, 1990

Fischer, Kathleen. *Winter Grace: Spirituality for Later Years*. New York: Paulist Press, 1985

Hauerwas, Stanley, Carole Bailey Stoneking, Keith G. Meador, and David Cloutier eds. *Growing Old in Christ*. Grand Rapids, Michigan. William B. Eerdmans Publishing Company, 2003

Hillman, James. *The Force of Character and the Lasting Life*. New York: Ballantine Books, 1999

Hollis, James. *On this Journey We Call Life: Living the Questions*. Toronto: Inner City Books, 2002

_____. *Finding Meaning in the Second Half of Life: How to Finally, Really Grow Up*. New York: Gotham Books, 2005

Jewel, Albert, ed. *Spirituality and Ageing*. London: Jessica Publishers, 1999

Kastenbaum, Robert, ed. *Old Age and the New Science*. New York: Springer Publishing Company, 1981

Kimble, Melvin A. and Susan H. McFadden, eds. *Aging, Spirituality and Religion: A Handbook Volume 2*. Minneapolis: Fortress Press, 2003

King, Robert H. and Elizabeth M. *Autumn Years: Taking the*

Contemplative Path. New York: Continuum, 2004

LeFevre, Carol and Perry LeFevre, eds. *Aging and the Human Spirit: A Reader in Religion and Gerontology.* Chicago: Exploration Press, 1985

Luce, Gay Gaer. *Longer Life, More Joy: Techniques for Enhancing Health, Happiness and Inner Vision.* North Hollywood, California: Newcastle Publishing Co., Inc., 1992

Luke, Helen M. *Old Age: Journey into Simplicity.* Waterville, Maine: Thorndike Press, 1987

Moody, Harry R. and David Carroll. *The Five Stages of Soul: Charting the Spiritual Passages that Shape our Lives.* New York: Anchor Books, 1998

Schachter-Shalomi, Zalman and Ronald S. Miller. *From Age-ing to Sage-ing: A Profound New Vision of Growing Older.* New York: WarnerBooks, 1995

Thibault, Jane Marie. *A Deepening Love Affair: The Gift of God in Later Life.* Nashville: Upper Room Books, 1993

Wagstrom-Halaas, Gwen. *Clergy, Retirement and Wholeness: Looking forward to the third age.* Herndon, VA: The Alban Institute, 2005

Walker, Barbara G. *The Crone: Woman of Age, Wisdom, and Power.* New York: HarperOne, 1985

Woodman, Marion. *The Crown of Age: The Rewards of Conscious Aging.* Boulder, Colorado: Sounds True CD, 2002

Dream Work

Bosnak, Robert. *A Little Course in Dreams.* Boston: Shambala, 1988

Johnson, Robert A. *Inner Work: Using Dreams and Active Imagination for Personal Growth,* New York: HarperSanFrancisco, 1986

Mellick, Jill. *The Art of Dreaming: Tools for Creative Dream Work.* Berkeley, California: Conari Press, 2001

Signell, Karen A. *Wisdom of the Heart: Working with Women's Dreams.* New York: Bantam Books, 1990

Woodman, Marion. *Dreams: Language of the Soul.* Cassette Recording No.A131. Boulder, Colorado: Sounds True Recordings, 1991

Mentoring

Clayton, Paul C. *Letters to Lee: Mentoring the New Minister.* Herndon, VA: The Alban Institute, 1999

Daloz, Laurent. *Mentor: Guiding the Journey of Adult Learners.* SanFrancisco: Jossey-Bass, 1999

Hendricks, Howard and William. *As Iron Sharpens Iron: Building Character in a Mentoring Relationship.* Chicago: Moody Press, 1995

Huang, Chungliang Al and Jerry Lynch. *Mentoring: The Tao of Giving and Receiving Wisdom.* San Francisco: HarperSanFrancisco, 1995

Joy, Donald M. *Empower Your Kids to be Adults: A Guide for Parents, Ministers, and Other Mentors.* Nappannee, Indiana: Evangel Publishing House, 2000

Rhodes, Jean E. *Stand By Me: The Risks and Rewards of Mentoring Today's Youth.* Cambridge, Massachusetts: Harvard University Press, 2002

Sellner, Edward C. *Mentoring: The Ministry of Spiritual Kinship*, Cambridge, Massachusetts: Cowley Publications, 2002

Simon, Henry. *Mentoring: A Tool for Ministry.* Saint Louis: Concordia Publishing House, 2001

Nature and Soul: Theory and Practice

Abram, David. *The Spell of the Sensuous: Perceptions and Language in a More-Than-Human World.* New York: Vintage Books, 1997

Endredy, James. *Earthwalks for Body and Spirit: Exercise to Restore Our Sacred Bond with The Earth.* Rochester, Vermont: Bear & Company, 2002

Foster, Stephen and Meredith Little. *The Four Shields: The Initiatory Seasons of Human Nature.* Big Pine, CA: Lost Borders Press, 1998

Heffern, Rich. *Adventures in Simple Living: A Creation-Centred Spirituality.* New York: Crossroads Publishing Company, 1994

Jensen, Derrick. *A Language Older Than Words.* White River Junction, Vermont: Chelsea Green Publishing Company, 2000

LaChapelle, Dolores. *Sacred Land Sacred Sex Rapture of the Deep: Concerning Deep Ecology and Celebrating Life*. Durango, Colorado: Kivaki Press, 1988

Macy, Joanna and Molly Young Brown. *Coming Back to Life: Practices to Reconnect our Lives Our World*. Gabriola Island, BC: New Society Publishers, 2000

McGaa, Ed. *Mother Earth Spirituality: Native American Paths to Healing Ourselves and our World*. New York: HarperSanFrancisco, 1990

Plotkin, Bill. *Soulcraft: Crossing into the Mysteries of Nature and Psyche*. Novato, California: New World Library, 2003

_____. *Nature and the Human Psyche: Cultivating Wholeness and Community in a Fragmented World*. Novato, California: New World Library, 2008

Scott, Susan S. *Healing with Nature*. New York: Helios Press, 2003

New Cosmology

Berry, Thomas. *The Great Work: Our Way Into the Future*. New York: Bell Tower, 1999

Conlon, James. *Earth Story Sacred Story*. Mystic, Connecticut: Twenty-Third Publications, 1994

O'Murchu, Diarmuid. *Quantum Theology: Spiritual Implications of the New Physics*. Crossroad Publishing Company, 1997

_____. *Evolutionary Faith: Rediscovering God in our Great Story*. Maryknoll, New York: Orbis Books, 2003

Rasmussen, Larry L. *Earth Community Earth Ethics*. Maryknoll, New York: Orbis Books, 1998

Sanguine, Bruce. *Darwin, Divinity and the Dance of the Cosmos: An Ecological Christianity*. Kelowna, BC: CopperHouse, 2007

Swimme, Brian. *The Hidden Heart of the Cosmos: Humanity and the New Story*. Maryknoll, NY: Orbis Books, 1996

Swimme, Brian and Thomas Berry. *The Universe Story: From the Primordial Flaring Forth to the Ecozoic Era—A Celebration of the Unfolding of the Cosmos*. New York: HarperCollins, 1992

Ritual

Black, Kathy and Heather Murray Elkins, eds. *Wising Up: Ritual Resources for Women of Faith in their Journey of Aging.* Cleveland, Ohio: The Pilgrim Press, 2005
Gilligan, Stephen, *The Courage to Love: Principles and Practices of Self-Relations Psychotherapy.* New York: W.W. Norton & Company, 1997
Somé, Patrice Malidoma. *The Healing Wisdom of Africa: Finding Life Purpose through Nature, Ritual and Community.* New York: Jeremy P. Tarcher/Putnam, 1999
van der Hart, O. *Rituals in Psychotherapy: Transition and Continuity.* New York: Irvington, 1983
_____. *Coping with Loss: The Therapeutic Use of Leave-Taking Rituals.* New York: Irvington, 1988

Soul Poetry

Berry, Thomas. *Collected Poems: 1952-1982.* New York: North Point Press, 1987
Crozier, Lorna. *What The Living Won't Let Go.* Toronto: McClelland and Stewart, 1999
_____. *Apocrypha of Light.* Toronto: McClelland & Stewart, 2002
Eliot, T. S., *Collected Poems 1909-1962.* 10th ed. New York: Harcourt, Brace & World Inc., 1970
Fox, John. *Finding What You Didn't Lose: Expressing Your Creativity Through Poem-Making.* New York: G.P. Putnam's Sons, 1995
Geddes, Gary, ed. *20th Century Poetry and Poetics.* Fourth Edition, Don Mills, Ontario: Oxford University Press, 1996
Oliver, Mary. *House of Light.* Boston: Beacon Press, 1990.
_____. *New and Selected Poems: Volume One.* Boston: Beacon Press, 1992
_____. *New and Selected Poems: Volume Two.* Boston: Beacon Press, 2005
MacLeish, Archibald. *Selected Poems 1926-1972.* Boston: Houghton Mifflin Company, 1973

Rilke, Rainer Maria. *The Selected Poetry of Rainer Maria Rilke.* ed. and trans. Stephen Mitchell, New York: Vintage Books, 1984.

_____. *Rilke's Book of Hours: Love Poems to God.* trans. Anita Barrows and Joanna Macy New York: Riverhead Books, 1996

Rumi. *The Soul of Rumi: A New Collection of Ecstatic Verse.* Trans. Coleman Barks. San Francisco: HarperSanFrancisco, 2001

Sewell, Marilyn, ed. *Claiming the Spirit Within: A Sourcebook of Women's Poetry.* Boston: Beacon Press, 1996

Whyte, David. *Fire in the Earth.* Langley, Washington: Many Rivers Press, 1992

_____. *The House of Belonging.* Langley, Washington: Many Rivers Press, 1997

_____. *The Heart Aroused: Poetry and the Preservation of the Soul in Corporate America.* New York: Currency Doubleday, 1994.

_____. *Crossing the Unknown Sea: Work as a Pilgrimage of Identity.* New York: Riverbend Books, 2001

Story

Baldwin, Christina. *Storycatcher: Making Sense of Our Lives through the Power and Practice of Story.* Novato, California: New World Library, 2005

Campbell, Joseph. *The Hero With a Thousand Faces.* Princeton, New Jersey: Princeton University Press, 1949, Third Princeton/Bollington Paperback, 1973

Chinen, Allan B. *In the Ever After: Fairy Tales and the Second Half of Life.* Wilmette, Illinois: Chirion Publications, 1989

_____. *Once Upon a Midlife: Classic Stories and Mythic Tales to Illuminate the Middle Years.* Xlibris Corporation, 2003

Dillard, Annie. *Pilgrim at Tinker Creek: A Mystical Excursion into Nature.* New York: Bantam, 1975

Estés, Clara Pinkola. *Women Who Run With the Wolves: Myths and Stories of the Wild Woman Archetype.* New York: Ballantyne Books, 1992

Hollis, James. *Mythologems: Incarnations of the Invisible World.* Toronto: Inner City Books, 2004

_____. *Tracking the Gods: The Place of Myth in Modern Life.* Toronto: Inner City Books, 1995

Kingsolver, Barbara. *Small Wonder.* New York: Perennial-Harper-Collins, 2003.

Metzger, Deena. *Writing for Your Life: A Guide and Companion to the Inner Worlds.* San Francisco: HarperSanFrancisco, 1992

Morgan, Richard L. *Remembering Your Story: Creating Your Own Spiritual Autobiography* Revised Edition. Nashville: Upper Room Books, 2002

Palmer, Parker J. *A Hidden Wholeness: The Journey Toward an Undivided Life.* San Francisco: Jossey-Bass, 2004

Prechtel, Martín. *The Disobedience of the Daughter of the Sun: Ecstasy and Time.* Cambridge, MA: Yellow Moon Press, 2001

Storm, Hyemeyohsts. "The Story of Jumping Mouse". www.ilhawaii.net/-stony/lore16html

Yolen, Jane. *Gray Heroes: Elder Tales from Around the World.* New York: Penguin Putnam, 1999

Theology and Faith

Bielecki, Tessa. *Holy Daring: An Outrageous gift to modern spirituality from Saint Teresa the grand wild woman of Avila.* Rockport, Massachusetts: Element, 1994

Boff, Leonardo. *Cry of the Earth, Cry of the Poor.* Maryknoll, New York: Orbis Books, 1997

Brueggemann, Walter. *The Prophetic Imagination.* Philadelphia: Fortress Press, 1978

_____. *Texts That Linger Words That Explode: Listening to Prophetic Voices.* Minneapolis: Fortress Press, 2000

Bruteau, Bernice. *The Grand Option: Personal Transformation and a New Creation.* Notre Dame, Indiana: Notre Dame University Press, 2001

Buechner, Frederick. *Wishful Thinking: A Theological ABC.* San Francisco: Harper & Row Publishers, 1973

Chittister, Joan D. *Heart of Flesh: A Feminist Spirituality for Women and Men.* Grand Rapids, Michigan: William B. Eerdmans Publishing, 1998

Chung, Hyun Kyung. *Struggle to be the Sun Again: Introducing Asian Women's Theology.* Maryknoll, New York: Orbis Books, 1997

Clifford, Anne M. *Introducing Feminist Theology.* Maryknoll, New York: Orbis Books, 2001

Ellison, Marvin. *Erotic Justice: A Liberating Ethic of Sexuality.*
Louisville, Kentucky: Westminster John Knox Press, 1996

Fox, Matthew. *Sins of the Spirit, Blessings of the Flesh.* New York:
Harmony Books, 1999

Gebara, Ivone. *Longing for Running Water: Ecofeminism and Liberation.*
Minneapolis: Fortress Press, 1999

Grey, Mary C. *Introducing Feminist Images of God.* Cleveland, Ohio:
The Pilgrim Press, 2001

_____. *Sacred Longings: The Ecological Spirit and Global Culture.*
Minneapolis: Fortress Press, 2004

Hallman, David G. *Spiritual Values for Earth Community.* Geneva:
WCC Publications, 2000

Harrison, Beverly Wildung. *Justice in the Making: Feminist Social
Ethics.* Louisville: Westminster John Knox Press, 2004

Heyward, Carter. *The Erotic as Power and the Love of God.* San
Francisco: Harper & Row, 1989

Hobgood, Mary Elizabeth. *Dismantling Privilege: An Ethics of
Accountability.* Cleveland: The Pilgrim Press, 2000.

Johnson, Elizabeth A. *Women, Earth, and Creator Spirit.* New York:
Paulist Press, 1993

_____. *She Who Is: The Mystery of God in Feminist Theological
Discourse.* New York: Crossroads Publishing Company, 1998

Jung, Shannon. *We Are Home: A Spirituality of the Environment.* New
York/Mahwah, N.J.: Paulist Press, 1993

Kidd, Sue Monk. *The Dance of the Dissident Daughter: A Woman's
Journey from Christian Tradition to the Sacred Feminine.* San
Francisco: HarperCollins, 1996.

Lanzetta, Beverly J. *Radical Wisdom: A Feminist Mystical Theology.*
Minneapolis: Fortress Press, 2005

Leddy, Mary Jo, *Radical Gratitude.* Maryknoll, New York: Orbis
Books, 2003

Marion, Jim, *Putting on the Mind of Christ: The Inner Work of Christian
Spirituality.* Charlottesville, VA: Hampton Roads
Publishing, 2000.

McFague, Sallie. *The Body of God: An Ecological Theology.*
Minneapolis: Fortress Press, 1993

_____. *Super, Natural Christians: How We Should Love Nature.*
Minneapolis: Fortress Press, 1997

_____. *Life Abundant: Rethinking Theology and Economy for a Planet in Peril.* Minneapolis: Fortress Press, 2001

Moore, Thomas. *The Soul's Religion: Cultivating a Profoundly Spiritual Way of Life.* New York, N.Y.: Perennial, 2002

Morwood, Michael. *Is Jesus God? Finding our Faith.* New York: The Crossroad Publishing Company, 2001

Muller, Wayne. *How Then Shall We Live?: Four Simple Questions that Reveal the Beauty And Meaning of Our Lives.* New York: Bantam Books, 1996.

Ochs, Carol. *Women and Spirituality.* Totowa, New Jersey: Rowman & Allanheld, 1983

O'Donohue, John. *beauty The Invisible Embrace.* New York: HarperCollins Publishers, 2004

Palmer, Parker, *Let Your Life Speak: Listening for the Voice of Vocation.* San Francisco: Jossey-Bass, 2000.

Plaskow, Judith and Carol P. Christ, eds. *Weaving the Visions: New Patterns in Feminist Spirituality.* New York: HarperSanFrancisco, 1989

Rasmussen, Larry L. *Earth Community Earth Ethics.* Maryknoll, New York: Orbis Books, 1998

Ruether, Rosemary Radford. *Women Healing Earth: Third World Women on Ecology, Feminism and Religion.* Maryknoll, New York: Orbis Books, 1996

Soelle, Dorothee. *On Earth as in Heaven: A Liberation Spirituality of Sharing,* Louisville, Kentucky: Westminster/John Knox Press, 1993

Wolman, Richard N. *Thinking With Your Soul: Spiritual Intelligence and Why It Matters.* New York, New York: Harmony Books, 2001

Notes:

Notes:

Made in the USA